Galaxy S7

&

S7 Edge

The 100% Unofficial User Guide

By Aaron J. Halbert

Version 1.0

Foreword

Thank you for purchasing *Samsung Galaxy S7 & S7 Edge: The 100% Unofficial User Guide*. I have worked hard to compile the most relevant and useful information for you, and I firmly believe that you will get your money's worth. Better yet, when you're finished with this book, your skills and knowledge will put you among the top 1% of power users.

If you have any feedback on this book, please email me at AJH@AaronHalbert.com or post a review on Amazon. By doing so, you'll help all users get the information they need, and you'll also have my gratitude. I carefully read and consider all the comments I receive, because I believe in listening to my customers.

A few things before we begin:

- This book covers both the S7 and S7 Edge. The two models have almost identical hardware and software, except for the S7 Edge's exclusive Edge Screen features. All Edge Screen-specific information is consolidated in Chapter 6 (p. 188), "The Edge Screen." All other sections of the book apply equally to both devices.
- Throughout this book I sometimes suggest you purchase apps or accessories to improve your Galaxy experience. I am <u>not</u> affiliated with any of these companies, nor do I receive any sort of compensation from them. All of my recommendations are based on my own experience and research. My opinion is not for sale.
- The best way to learn from this book is to follow along on your own device. You'll learn much faster by going through the motions yourself. Reading from start to finish is not mandatory, but active participation is extremely helpful for remembering what you read.

Contents at a Glance

Detailed Contents

Chapter 1: Introduction

Thank you for purchasing *Samsung Galaxy S7 & S7 Edge: The 100% Unofficial User Guide*! This book is designed to help you unlock the potential of your Galaxy regardless of your previous Android experience. If you're brand new to Android, I'll explain everything from the ground up. If you already know your way around an Android device, you can easily skip to the intermediate and advanced chapters.

Structure of This Book

Chapter 2, About the S7 & S7 Edge (p. 19), briefly tells the history of the Galaxy S series. In this chapter, I explain what's new and exciting with the S7 and S7 Edge.

Chapter 3, Getting Started (p. 24), guides you through initial setup to get your Galaxy up and running fast.

Chapter 4, Fundamentals for New Users (p. 54), is a crash course for first-time Android users. It covers fundamental topics such as the home screen, the lock screen, and the notification panel.

Chapter 5, Basic Functions (p. 88), teaches you how to perform everyday tasks on your Galaxy such as making calls, sending emails, sending text messages, taking photos, navigating using the GPS, installing apps, and more.

Chapter 6, The Edge Screen (p. 188), is a special chapter dedicated to the S7 Edge. It provides an overview of the S7 Edge's unique Edge Screen features and includes detailed usage instructions.

Chapter 7, Intermediate Tips & Tricks (p. 201), helps you take your Galaxy to the next level with customizations and tweaks. For example, you'll learn how to encrypt your SD card, how to pair Bluetooth devices, how to block unwanted calls, how to print documents, and much more.

Chapter 8, Advanced Functions (p. 272), covers power-user topics such as rooting your Galaxy, programming and using NFC tags, and connecting USB devices such as flash drives and mice.

Chapter 9, Preloaded Apps (p. 287), provides brief summaries and reviews of apps that come pre-loaded on the S7 and S7 Edge. In some cases, I point you toward better alternatives.

In Chapter 10, The 50 All-Time Best Android Apps (p. 296), I recommend my 50 most-used third-party apps (i.e., apps that do *not* come pre-loaded, but are available from the

Google Play Store and other sources). This chapter contains something for everyone. It's a book-within-a-book; this information is normally sold separately on Amazon as the book *The 50 All-Time Best Android Apps*, but I've included it all here in Chapter 10, 100% free, as a way of saying "thanks" for your purchase.

Finally, in Chapter 11, Accessory Shopping Guide (p. 311), I discuss the types of accessories available for the S7 and S7 Edge, provide examples, and make some recommendations.

Why Buy This Book?

Although it's possible to learn your Galaxy's features by experimenting, it's a lot easier and faster to use this book. It consolidates everything you need to know in one place and presents the information in a logical and sequential order that you won't find anywhere else.

In this book, I tell you how each and every app and feature works, but I don't stop there. I also tell you which are worthwhile and which are gimmicks. I suggest third-party alternatives that I trust. You will benefit from my years of experience with Android and other mobile platforms.

Other authors might assume that you already understand core concepts, leading to confusion and frustration. On the other hand, I try to make as few assumptions as possible, and explain everything from the ground up in plain English. All you need is a basic knowledge of computers and browsing the Internet.

You can read this book cover-to-cover or just open it to the page you need. Use the Detailed Table of Contents (p. 5) to quickly find what you're looking for. Electronic editions of this book contain hundreds of clickable bookmarks (underlined text) so you can easily skip around the book and read more about topics of interest. Paper editions contain page numbers in place of clickable bookmarks.

Simply put, if you are a brand new Android user and you don't know the Play Store from the App Drawer, this book teaches you from first principles. If you already know and love Android, this book teaches you all the particular ins and outs of your new S7 or S7 Edge.

Who Am I?

Who am I, and what are my qualifications?

First, I am a bestselling tech author. Some of my previous books include:

- *Samsung Galaxy Note 5 and S6 Edge+: The 100% Unofficial User Guide*
- *Samsung Galaxy S6 and S6 Edge: The 100% Unofficial User Guide*

- *Samsung Galaxy S5: The 100% Unofficial User Guide*
- *Samsung Galaxy Note 4: The 100% Unofficial User Guide*
- *Samsung Galaxy Note 3: The 100% Unofficial User Guide*, and
- *Unlock the Power of Your Chromecast.*

Check them out on my Amazon author page:

> *http://www.amazon.com/Aaron-Halbert/e/B00H20GKF0/*
>
> *(Short link: http://goo.gl/D7fdlb)*

More importantly, I am an Android enthusiast just like you. I have owned and used more than 15 different Android devices since Android first hit the market in 2008 on the T-Mobile G1. I have pushed each one to its limits, both in stock and rooted configurations, and I have taught countless others to do the same. In the decade before Android hit the market, I used numerous Windows Mobile and Palm OS phones and PDAs. In fact, I got my first one in 2002. I have written for several enthusiast websites, including one popular one that I started, owned, and ran in the early 2000s. This ain't my first rodeo.

The possibilities offered by devices like the S7 and S7 Edge are amazing. The first smartphones were little more than glorified day planners; today, your Galaxy can do nearly anything that your desktop computer can.

To make the most of your new phone, read this book.

Chapter 2: About the S7 & S7 Edge

Summary of Features

Evolution, Not Revolution

Samsung is a powerful force in today's smartphone world. In fact, it's *the* biggest manufacturer of Android smartphones, and the second biggest manufacturer of smartphones overall. The only company that sells more smartphones than Samsung is Apple. To provide some perspective, the market research firm comScore reported in March 2016 that Apple controlled 43% of the smartphone market, with Samsung at 28% and the distant-third-place LG at 10%.

But things weren't always this way. In fact, it wasn't until 2010, when Samsung released the first Galaxy S, that it achieved real success in the smartphone market. Every year since then, Samsung has packed its best technology into one phone and released it as a new Galaxy S. Since 2010, Samsung has sold hundreds of millions of Galaxy S2, S3, S4, S5, and S6 units. In this way, the Galaxy S7 and S7 Edge are the latest entries in history's most successful line of Android phones. They're kind of a big deal.

There aren't any groundbreaking new features in the S7 and S7 Edge, but I'd argue that's a good thing. Instead of dramatically innovating, the S7 and S7 Edge improve upon the already-successful S6 and S6 Edge, which are often considered the pinnacle of the Galaxy S series thanks to their impressive performance and premium glass-and-metal chassis. The S7 and S7 Edge aim to address the weaknesses of the S6 and S6 Edge such as limited battery life, lack of a MicroSD memory card slot, and lack of waterproofing.

Here's a quick summary of what's new and exciting with the S7 and S7 Edge:

- **Sturdy Build Quality:** Unlike early Samsung phones that were made of plastic, the S7 or S7 Edge are all glass and metal. The phones' fronts and backs are made of durable, scratch- and shatter-resistant Corning Gorilla Glass 4 and their bezels are aluminum alloy. Samsung first introduced this design with the original S6 and S6 Edge to compete with the Apple iPhone, and has carried it over to the S7 and S7 Edge. There's no doubt that these are the best-looking and sturdiest Samsung smartphones yet.
- **Premium Specs:** The S7 and S7 Edge are Samsung's most powerful smartphones to date. Samsung has increased total RAM to 4 GB on both phones and packed in the latest 64-bit Snapdragon/Exynos processors. Translation? Super snappy performance.

- **Best-Ever Screens:** The S7 and S7 Edge feature 5.1" and 5.5" Super AMOLED screens respectively, both with 2560 x 1440-pixel resolution. The S6 and S6 Edge had the same resolution, but the panels in the S7 and S7 Edge have been qualitatively improved for even brighter colors and better contrast. Note that the S7 and S7 Edge have screens of different sizes, with the S7 Edge's screen being 0.4" larger than the S7's. This is a change from the S6 and S6 Edge, which had identically sized screens.

- **A Camera Designed for Low-Light Shots**: The rear camera on the S7 and S7 Edge features dual-pixel technology, making it the best low-light smartphone camera ever. It's also got a wider field of view, faster autofocus, and protrudes less from the back of the phone. It's got all the other goodies, too, like optical image stabilization as well as RAW support for the Adobe Lightroom enthusiasts among us. Note that the number of megapixels has actually *decreased* due to the dual-pixel technology—but don't be misled—more megapixels isn't always better. The S7 and S7 Edge take slightly smaller pictures than the S6/S6 Edge with their 16 MP sensors, but the image quality is better. The trade-off is worth it.

- **Bigger Batteries and Powered-Up Battery Charging**: The S7 and S7 Edge innovate on battery charging in several ways. First, they feature Adaptive Fast Charging, which, according to Samsung, provides four hours of juice in 10 minutes of wired charging. Second, they have built-in compatibility with all industry-standard Qi and PMA wireless charging pads, which can be purchased for about $20. Third, and even better, both phones are also compatible with Samsung's Fast Charge wireless pad (~$70), which wirelessly charge a completely dead battery in just two hours—significantly faster than Qi or PMA. Finally, the built-in batteries in both the S7 and S7 Edge have higher capacities than ever before, meaning your phone lasts longer on each charge.

- **Water Resistance:** The Galaxy S5 boasted water resistance, but this feature disappeared on the S6 and S6 Edge. It's back on the S7 and S7 Edge and better than ever. All the rubber gaskets are located *inside* the phone, which means no clumsy rubber stoppers around external ports. These devices are water resistant in up to 5 feet of water for 30 minutes.

- **MicroSD Memory Card Slot:** This is another feature that temporarily disappeared on the S6 and S6 Edge but returns with the S7. With the S6 and S6 Edge, you were limited to the base memory that came with the phone—there was no way to add a memory card to store more photos, music, or video. The S7 and S7 Edge once again feature MicroSD slots so you can easily add cheap storage to your device. Cards up to 200GB are supported.

- **New Edge Screen Features (S7 Edge Only):** Samsung has reworked the S7 Edge's Edge Screen features, and claims they're now more useful and refined than ever.

- **Always-On Display:** The S7 and S7 Edge feature a new always-on screen option. You can set your device to display basic information like the time, date, calendar, and/or your notifications at all times, even while the device is asleep. Better yet, this feature only uses about 1% battery power per hour.

- **Android Marshmallow Features:** Both the S7 and S7 Edge run the newest version of the Android OS, Marshmallow. This means you get features like:
    - **Now On Tap:** Now On Tap reads the contents of your screen and provides useful quick-actions that it thinks you might like to take. For example, if Now On Tap finds the name of a local restaurant on your screen, it provides a shortcut to call the restaurant, a shortcut to navigate to it, and so on.
    - **Doze:** Automatically puts your device into deep sleep when it's not being used. With Doze, Google says you can expect your phone to lose only 3-5% of its battery power overnight. Anyone who's ever woken up to a dead phone will definitely appreciate the improvements Google's made with Doze. Better yet, Doze is all automatic—you don't need to turn it on. It just works in the background.
    - **App Standby:** Prevents seldom-used apps from draining your battery power in the background.
    - **Permissions Control:** More specific control over each apps' permissions. For example, if an app requests permission to use your phone's camera or GPS, you now have a choice whether or not to allow it.
    - **Encrypted Data by Default:** In previous versions of Android, you could encrypt the data on your phone, but you had to follow a time-consuming procedure. You also had to know it was possible in the first place, which many people didn't. Not so on the S7 and S7 Edge. At a time when the merits of data encryption are being widely debated in the United States, Google has switched on encryption by default. Should your S7 or S7 Edge ever fall into the wrong hands, you can be assured your data will be completely secure.

- **Top-Notch Fingerprint Sensor:** The S7 and S7 Edge have a fingerprint sensor built into the ⬭ button. To use it, you just place your thumb on ⬭ for about half a second, and it verifies your identity. It's integrated with several features on the S7, including the lock screen, Samsung Pay, and more.

- **Samsung Pay:** This is my personal favorite. Not only can you use your S7 or S7 Edge to pay at tap-to-pay checkouts, you can also use it with regular magnetic swipe terminals. Yes, that means that anywhere you can swipe a credit card, you can use your phone—wirelessly. There's no catch; just wireless magnetic wizardry. It's pretty amazing technology.

Of course, the S7 and S7 Edge also carry over plenty of other classic Samsung features, like S Health (p. 243), Download Booster (p. 234), a heart rate sensor (p. 247), ultra power saving mode (p. 239), and more. Samsung has also improved TouchWiz (p. 54), the custom interface it layers atop the core Android OS. You'll learn all about these features throughout this book.

What's Missing

Despite all the improvements made to the S7 and S7 Edge, there are a few missing features.

- **No USB-C:** USB-C is a new type of USB port. Like the conventional Micro USB port on the S7 and S7 Edge, USB-C is used for 1) charging and 2) transferring data. However, USB-C allows faster data transfer, has a symmetrical plug, and can be used for reverse-charging other devices—among other benefits. At a time when many new Android devices are shipping with USB-C, Samsung has opted not to include it on the S7 and S7 Edge.

- **No Removable Battery:** Unfortunately, the S7 and S7 Edge's batteries are sealed and can't be swapped out when you're running low on power. This drawback is mitigated by the S7 and S7 Edge's excellent battery life and quick charging times, but nothing compares to going from 0% to 100% by popping in a spare battery.

- **No IR Blaster:** Previous Galaxy S models featured an infrared port to let your phone function as a TV remote control. This feature has been removed from the S7 and S7 Edge.

- **No Storage Options Larger Than 32GB:** Models with 64GB and 128GB of built-in storage aren't available—only 32GB. If you need more memory to store photos, music, or videos, your only option is to add a MicroSD card.

- **No MHL-to-HDMI Support:** Many previous Samsung phones supported MHL-to-HDMI adapters, which allowed you to connect your phone to your HDTV to play video on the big screen. The S7 and S7 Edge don't support this feature.

Specifications

The table below shows the hardware specifications of the S7 and S7 Edge alongside those of the S6 and S6 Edge.

	S7/S7 Edge	S6/S6 Edge
Size	142.5 x 69.6 x 7.9 mm / 148.6 x 72.4 x 7.6 mm	143.4 x 70.5 x 6.8 mm / 142.1 x 70.1 x 7 mm
Weight	152g / 157g	138g / 132g
Screen	5.1" / 5.5" Quad HD Super AMOLED (2,560 x 1,440)	5.1" Quad HD Super AMOLED (2,560 x 1,440)
Storage	32 GB (with microSD slot)	32, 64, 128 GB (no microSD)
Processor	Snapdragon or Exynos, depends on region	Cortex-A53 & Cortex-A57
RAM	4GB	3GB
Camera	12MP Dual Pix. + OIS, 5MP Front	16MP+OIS, 5MP Front
Battery	3,000 mAh (fixed) / 3,600 mAh (fixed)	2,550 mAh (fixed) / 2,600 mAh (fixed)

Chapter 3: Getting Started

Device Anatomy

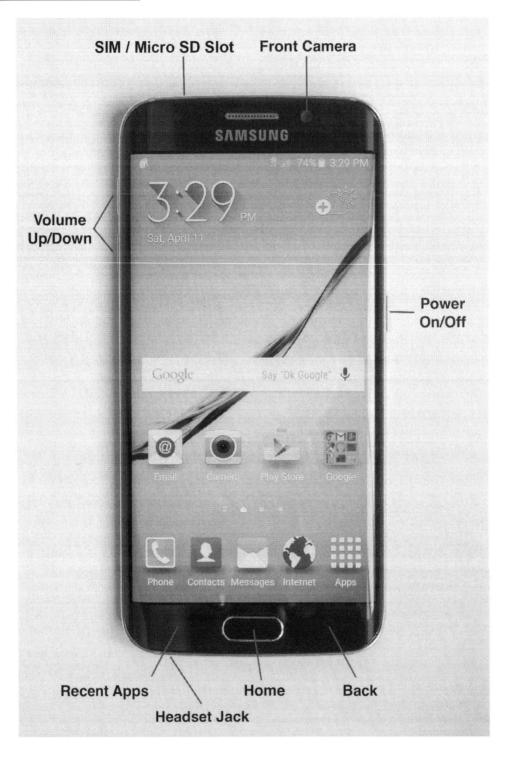

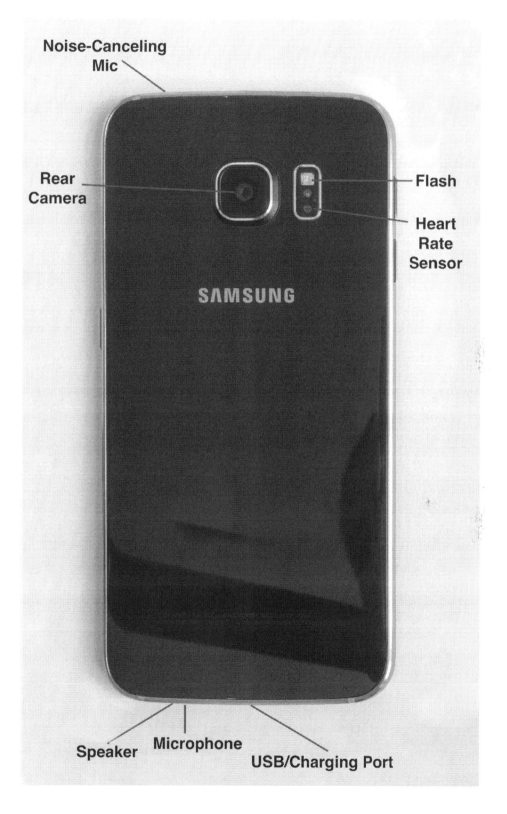

Noise-Canceling Mic

Rear Camera

Flash

Heart Rate Sensor

Speaker Microphone

USB/Charging Port

Initial Hardware Setup

What's a SIM Card?

- Before using your new Galaxy, you need to install a SIM card.
- What's a SIM card? It's a small, removable chip that contains your cell account information and lets your Galaxy connect to your carrier's cellular network.
- If you purchased your Galaxy brand new in a store, the salesperson probably installed and activated your SIM for you. If your Galaxy rings when you call it, then your SIM is already installed and you can skip this section.

TIP: A few years ago, CDMA networks like Sprint and Verizon didn't require SIM cards. However, this has changed with the introduction of 4G LTE. Your Galaxy requires a SIM card regardless of which carrier you have.

- The S7 and S7 Edge use nano-SIM cards, which are smaller than older mini-SIM and micro-SIM cards.
- If your previous phone used a nano-SIM card, you're in luck because you can just swap your old card into your new Galaxy using the instructions below and it'll start working immediately. If you're not sure, remove your SIM from your old phone (consult its instruction manual) and see if it fits your Galaxy's SIM tray. If yes, it's a nano-SIM and you're good to go. But if not, you need to get a new nano-SIM and call customer service to request a new SIM activation.
- Note that many carriers include a free nano-SIM card with new phones, so check your Galaxy's box before going to a carrier store to purchase one.

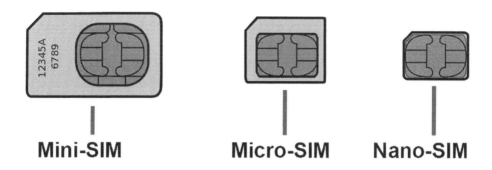

Mini-SIM   **Micro-SIM**   **Nano-SIM**

- It's also possible to convert a mini-SIM or micro-SIM card to nano-SIM with a SIM cutting tool and sandpaper (really, no joke!)—but not necessarily cheaper or easier than getting a new nano-SIM.

- I don't really recommend this method unless you know what you're doing and you have a reason not to simply get a new nano-SIM. Proceed with caution if you choose to cut down your old SIM card! Search Google for instructions if you want to try this method.

What's a Micro SD Card?

- A SIM card is required, but a Micro SD card is optional.

- While a SIM card contains your cell account information, a Micro SD card adds additional storage capacity to your phone's memory so it can store more data like music, photos, and videos. The S7 and S7 Edge come with 32GB of internal storage—not a small amount—but you might be surprised how quickly it fills up, especially if you take a lot of photos and video with your phone's camera.

- Since Micro SD cards are dirt cheap these days (~$10 for a 32GB card), I suggest picking one up. See <u>Chapter 11</u> (p. 311) for more information about buying appropriate Micro SD cards. You can install a Micro SD card at any time, so don't sweat it if you don't have one to install now.

Nano-SIM / Micro SD Installation Instructions

Follow these steps to install your nano-SIM and Micro SD cards. See below for helpful photographs of the process. It's not necessary to power off your Galaxy beforehand.

- If purchased new, your Galaxy comes wrapped in protective plastic. Don't peel it off yet; leave it on to protect your phone while you install your nano-SIM and Micro SD cards.

- Locate the SIM tray removal tool that comes in the box. It's a small metal tool with a protruding pin.

- Insert the pin into the SIM card slot's pinhole release, and gently push until the SIM card tray pops out. Pull it the rest of the way out with your fingertips.

- Place your nano-SIM and Micro SD cards into the tray, and re-insert the tray into your Galaxy. Make sure the orientation of the cards matches the tray. The metal pins on the nano-SIM card should face down, opposite the screen. If you have trouble re-inserting the SIM tray, stop and double check the orientation of both parts. Don't force the tray or you may damage your Galaxy.

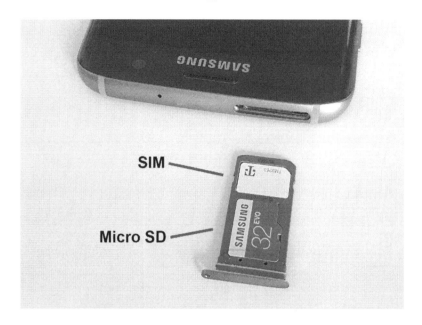

Now, remove the protective plastic film from your Galaxy's screen.

Initial Software Setup

- After you've completed the nano-SIM and Micro SD installation process, plug in your Galaxy using the supplied power adapter and cable.
- An orange-red LED light on the front upper-left-hand corner of the phone illuminates, indicating the device is charging.
- Turn on the Galaxy by pressing and holding the power button on the upper-right-hand edge of the device.
- After the device powers up for the first time, this screen appears:

- On this screen, select your preferred language by scrolling through the language list with one finger.
- Tap "Accessibility" if you're hard of seeing or hearing to set up some <u>accessibility features</u> (p. 221) like hearing aid support, text vocalization, and screen magnification.
- Otherwise, tap "Start" to proceed to the Wi-Fi configuration screen.

Connecting to Wi-Fi

- If you have a Wi-Fi Internet connection available, tap 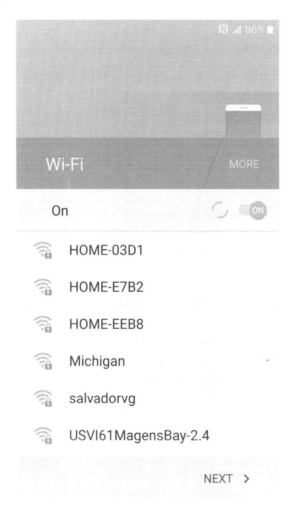 to power on your Wi-Fi connection.
- Your Galaxy searches for available Wi-Fi networks and displays them in a list as shown below.

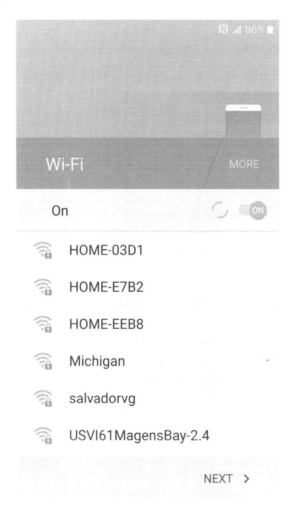

⭐ **TIP:** *If your carrier supports Wi-Fi Calling, you may see a message about it during Wi-Fi setup. Just tap "Skip" to dismiss the message. Wi-Fi Calling lets you make and receive calls any time your Galaxy is connected to a Wi-Fi network, even when outside of cell range. If your carrier supports Wi-Fi calling, it's enabled by default and works automatically without any additional setup on your part. Consult your carrier if you're unsure if it offers Wi-Fi Calling.*

- Tap the name of your preferred network.

- You are prompted to enter your network's WEP/WPA password. Do so and tap "Connect."
- If successful, a dialog box appears that says "Wi-Fi Connected." Tap "OK" and then "Next."
- If you enter an incorrect password, you are prompted to re-enter it.
- If your router has a WPS button (⏻), you can use it to quickly connect without entering a password. Tap "More" → "WPS push button." Then, press the ⏻ button on your wireless router and your Galaxy connects automatically.
- If you don't have a Wi-Fi connection available, tap "Next" and the Galaxy uses your carrier's wireless data connection instead. This may count against your cell plan's data quota, depending on your service plan. I recommend using Wi-Fi when possible.

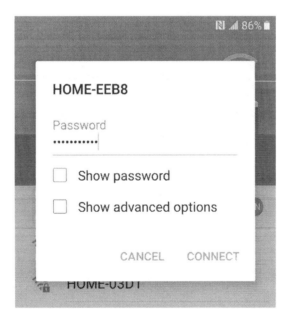

⭐ **TIP:** *If your Galaxy won't let you proceed without connecting to Wi-Fi first, it's because it doesn't yet have a cellular data connection. Give it a few minutes, or move elsewhere if you're in an area with poor cell coverage. You'll be able to proceed without a Wi-Fi connection after a cellular connection has been established.*

Accepting the Terms and Conditions

- Next, you're prompted to read Samsung's EULA (End User Licensing Agreement). Tap "Learn more" if you actually want to read it—but be warned, it's just a giant and boring legal document—the same kind you get when installing most any software. Since you can't proceed without accepting it, anyway, save yourself the time and don't bother.

- The "Diagnostic data" checkbox lets Samsung collect anonymous usage data to improve its software. I personally untick this checkbox because it can slightly improve battery life.

- Tap "Next" and then "Agree" to accept the EULA and continue setup.

Terms and conditions

End User License Agreement

Read the End User License Agreement carefully. It contains important information.

Learn more

Diagnostic data

☐ agree to (i) the automatic transmit of diagnostic and usage data and (ii) the collection, use, storage, sharing and disclosure by Samsung of diagnostic and usage data from your device for the purposes set out above.

NEXT ›

- After tapping "Next," your Galaxy verifies your Internet connection and checks for over-the-air (OTA) software updates.

- If one is available, proceed through the dialog boxes to install it.

> ⭐ **TIP:** *At some point during the setup process, you're prompted to enable Google's app verification service. Make sure you tap "Accept." Verify Apps is an official Google feature that runs in the background and protects your Galaxy from harmful and invasive applications. If a problem app is detected, you are notified and prompted to remove it.*

Sometimes, this prompt doesn't appear until after the setup process, when you try to install an app from the Google Play Store.

> Allow Google to regularly check device activity for security problems, and prevent or warn about potential harm.
>
> Learn more in the Google Settings app.
>
> DECLINE   ACCEPT

Transferring Data from Your Old Android Device Using Tap & Go

- Next, you're prompted to transfer data from a previous Android device using Google's "Tap & Go" data restore feature.

- Tap & Go copies over your Google account, installed apps, Wi-Fi passwords, and system settings from your previous Android device with minimal hassle. It does *not* transfer Gallery photos or text messages, which are copied separately, later in the setup process.

- Tap & Go only works if your old device supports NFC (common on phones made in the last 3-4 years). Consult your old device's instruction manual or search Google to determine if it supports NFC.

Got another device?

If you use another Android device, you can quickly copy your current setup to this SM-G935T.

○   Copy your Google Accounts, apps, and data from your other device

○   No thanks

‹   NEXT ›

- To proceed, enable NFC in your old device's system settings (again, consult its instruction manual) and ensure the device is turned on and unlocked. Select "Copy your Google Accounts…" and tap "Next."

- Place your old device back-to-back with your new Galaxy until you hear a tone. Separate the devices and then follow the prompts on both devices to initiate the data transfer.

- If you don't want to use Tap & Go, select "No thanks" and then "Next." There are two main reasons you might not want to use Tap & Go: 1) This is your first Android device and you don't have another one from which to copy data. 2) You want to set up your new device fresh instead of copying your old data.

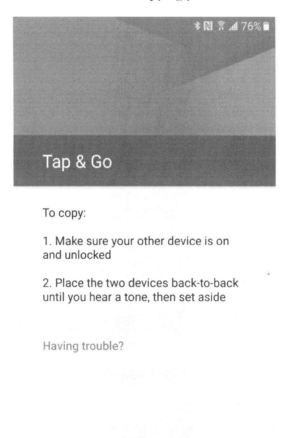

- After the process is complete, you're prompted to enable a few settings like data backup and location services.

Google services

These services put Google to work for you, and you can turn them on or off at any time for your aaronh123987@gmail.com account. Data will be used in accordance with Google's Privacy Policy.

☑ **Automatically back up device data** (such as Wi-Fi passwords and call history) and app data (such as settings and files stored by apps) to Google Drive. Learn more

- On this screen, scroll with one finger to see all available options. Personally, I leave all the boxes checked, with the exception of "Help improve your Android experience," which I disable for potential battery life benefits.

- Some readers have asked me if these settings, especially the location settings, are privacy threats since they send potentially sensitive information to Google.

- This is a complicated discussion outside the scope of this chapter, but to make a long story short, my judgment is that they are not. While I do not claim that any big company like Google is entirely benevolent, I don't believe that Google is interested in meddling with your personal affairs. Rather, Google is interested in gathering your data to serve you with better information and to improve its own products. Besides, let's be frank: if the NSA orders Google to monitor you, unchecking these boxes isn't going to stop them. When using a smartphone in the 21st century, you pretty much have to accept that big companies or the government can see your data if they want to. If data privacy is extremely important to you, you should rethink the idea of using a smartphone in the first place.

- So, my opinion is that there's little point in crippling your Galaxy's features by disabling these services. Leave them enabled and enjoy the benefits like automatic data restoration, improved local searches, Google Now customization, and more. By disabling them you lose some pretty useful features and gain little in the way of privacy.

Signing into Your Existing Google Account Without Using Tap & Go

- If you skip Tap & Go, you're prompted to sign into an existing Google account with your username and password. You want to sign in this way if you *do* have an existing Google account, but you:
  - o Can't use Tap & Go because your old Android doesn't support NFC,
  - o Or you don't want to copy over your old data,
  - o Or your new Galaxy is your first Android device!
- If you don't have a Google account, then skip to the next section: Creating a New Google Account (p. 40).

>  **TIP:** Not sure if you have a Google account? If you have a Gmail address, you have a Google account—your username is the part that comes before "@gmail.com."

- To sign in, enter your Gmail address or username and tap "Next."

- Enter your password when prompted, and then tap "Accept" to confirm and sign in.
- Finally, you configure Google services. Swipe down using one finger to see the available options. As mentioned above in the Tap & Go section, I recommend enabling everything except "Help improve your Android experience."
- Tap "Next" to continue.

Google services

These services put Google to work for you, and you can turn them on or off at any time for your aaronh123987@gmail.com account. Data will be used in accordance with Google's Privacy Policy.

☑ **Automatically back up device data** (such as Wi–Fi passwords and call history) and app data (such as settings and files stored by apps) to Google Drive. Learn more

<   ⌄

- You may see a screen like the following, prompting you to restore apps from a previous Android device. Choose the device and apps you wish to automatically restore by tapping the dropdown menus below "Restore from this backup" and "Also include," and then tap "Next" to continue. Note that this screen displays the model number of your last Android phone, rather than its name (for example, SM-G935T instead of "Galaxy S7"). If you have multiple devices linked to your Google account and you don't recognize the model number, Google it to find out which device it is.

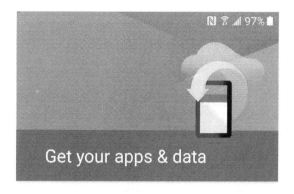

Easily set up your new device by
restoring from a backup of another
device.

Backups include apps, app data,
system settings and Wi-Fi passwords.

Restore from this backup

SM-G935T Last used today ▼

Also include

All apps 26 ▼

< NEXT >

Creating a New Google Account

- If you don't have a Google account (meaning, you don't have a Gmail address), tap "Or create a new account" when you reach this screen:

Add your account   ⋮

Google

Sign in to get the most out of your device.

Enter your email

Need help finding your account?

Or create a new account

- **If you don't already have a Google account, create one now. I cannot over-emphasize the importance of doing so.**
- Android is a Google product and many of the Galaxy's features require you to have a Google account. If you don't, you won't be able to download any new apps from the Google Play Store, automatically back up your contacts, sync your bookmarks and passwords through Chrome, automatically back up your photos to Google Photos, or take advantage of many other useful features that I'll discuss throughout this book.
- Even if you don't use Gmail for email, you should still create a Google account to take advantage of the many other features a Google account adds to your Galaxy.
- When creating a Google account, you specify a username (the part of your email address that comes before "@gmail.com") and password, your real name, and set up a phone number for emergency recovery of your account password. I recommend using your Galaxy's phone number for this.

First name

Last name

You'll use this username to sign in to
your Google Account

Username   @gmail.com

Only use A-Z, a-z, and 0-9

Create password

At least 8 characters

Confirm password

By continuing, you agree to the
Privacy Policy and Terms of Service.

Don't create the account

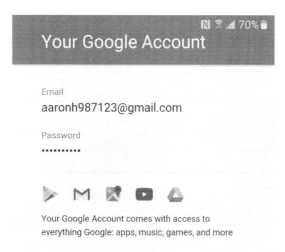

- Next, you're prompted to configure Google services. I recommend leaving everything enabled except "Help improve your Android experience."

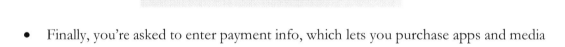

Google services

These services put Google to work for you, and you can turn them on or off at any time for your aaronh123987@gmail.com account. Data will be used in accordance with Google's Privacy Policy.

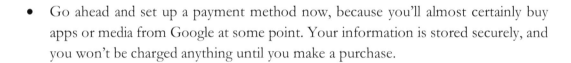

Automatically back up device data (such as Wi-Fi passwords and call history) and app data (such as settings and files stored by apps) to Google Drive. Learn more

- Finally, you're asked to enter payment info, which lets you purchase apps and media on the Google Play Store.
- Go ahead and set up a payment method now, because you'll almost certainly buy apps or media from Google at some point. Your information is stored securely, and you won't be charged anything until you make a purchase.

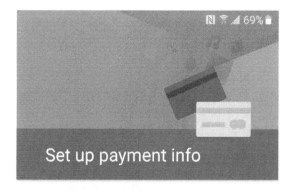

Set up payment info

Enter your billing information. **You won't be charged unless you make a purchase.**

◉ Add credit or debit card

○ Add PayPal

○ Redeem code

○ No thanks

⟨ CONTINUE ⟩

Setting the Date & Time

- After signing into or creating your Google account, you're prompted to adjust your Galaxy's date and time settings.
- Generally, your Galaxy automatically sets the date and time based on your carrier's network settings. If the date & time are incorrect, then adjust them and tap "Next" to continue.

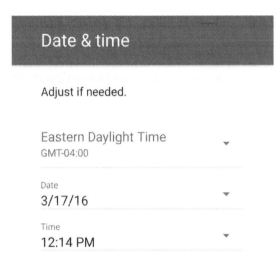

Adding Additional Email Addresses

- Next, you're prompted to register any additional email addresses you may have, so that you can send & receive emails from those accounts using your Galaxy.
- This step is completely optional.
- If you wish to register additional email addresses, select "Personal (IMAP/POP) and tap "Next." Follow the prompts to complete the process.
- Otherwise, select "Not now" and tap "Next" to continue.

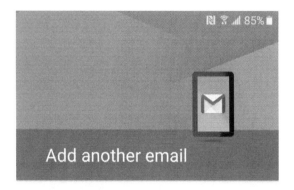

aaronh123987@gmail.com is ready.

If you also use a personal or Exchange email address, you can add it now.

○   Personal (IMAP/POP)
    Yahoo, Outlook.com, etc.

○   Not now
    Add later in Gmail app

Configuring Your Lock Screen

- Next, you're prompted to configure your lock screen (p. 206), which protects your Galaxy from unauthorized use with your choice of a password, fingerprint scan, etc. When enabled, the lock screen appears every time your Galaxy is powered on, preventing anyone from using your phone without first authenticating themselves.

- You can read a detailed comparison of lock screen methods here (p. 206), but I strongly suggest using fingerprint recognition. The S7 and S7 Edge have excellent fingerprint sensors that just require a quick tap of your thumb on the button—much quicker and easier than entering a PIN or password.
- Tap "Set up fingerprint" and follow the instructions to register your fingerprint and set up a backup PIN, password, or pattern.

Configuring Lock Screen Notification Privacy

- Next, you see this screen. Understanding these settings requires a bit of background knowledge about the lock screen.

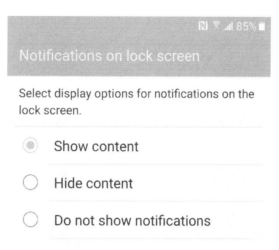

- Normally, when your Galaxy sends you a notification (to alert you of a new text message, email, etc.) it displays that notification on the lock screen while your Galaxy is locked. This is convenient because you can just tap the power button to read the notification, without having to authenticate yourself first.

- However, some people may not want any personal information to be displayed on the lock screen. So, these settings let you control what information your Galaxy is permitted to show on the lock screen.

- To show some potentially sensitive info on the lock screen for the sake of convenience, select "Show content."

- To only display redacted notifications on the lock screen (i.e., to show you the type of notification, but without any personal info like sender or subject line), select "Hide Content."

- To block all notifications on the lock screen, select "Do not show notifications."

- This is a personal decision about convenience vs. privacy—it's convenient to see notifications directly on your lock screen without having to authenticate yourself— but if your phone was ever lost or stolen, would you be okay with a stranger seeing snippets of your text messages, emails, and other notifications?

- After choosing your desired setting, tap "Next" to continue.

Creating or Logging into a Samsung Account

- Next, you're prompted to create a Samsung account, which grants you access to the Samsung Galaxy Apps store and provides some useful data backup features.

- In previous *100% Unofficial User Guides*, I recommended against creating a Samsung account because it worked clumsily, did little that a Google account didn't already do, and increased battery drain. However, Samsung accounts are more efficient and functional these days and I now recommend creating one. The most useful features of a Samsung account are:
  - o Backing up phone logs and text messages
  - o Backing up and syncing S Health fitness data
  - o Backing up system settings
  - o Downloading apps and updates from the Galaxy Apps Store, including themes

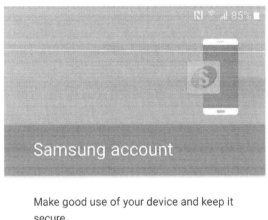

- To create a Samsung account, tap "Create Account" and enter the necessary information to create your Samsung account and sign in. Agree to Samsung's terms and conditions. If you are prompted to enable backup features, do so.

- If you don't want a Samsung account, tap "Skip" on the initial Samsung account screen.

- If you already have a Samsung account, tap "Sign in" and follow the prompts to restore data from your Samsung account.

- Check here (p. 262) for a complete tutorial on backing up your Galaxy's data.

- ⭐ *TIP: If you skip creating a Samsung account during initial device setup and change your mind, you can always create one later. Do so in system settings → "Accounts" → "Add account."*

Copying Photos and Text Messages from Your Old Phone

Next, you're prompted to copy photos and text messages from your old phone.

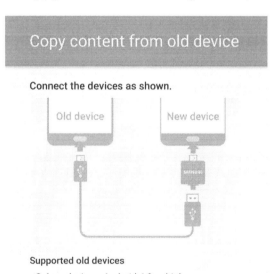

- To do so, use the USB cable and Micro USB adapter that came in your S7's box to connect the two devices. The transfer process starts automatically. Follow all prompts to complete it.

- If you don't want to transfer photos and text messages, tap "Later."

Easy Mode—Skip It

- Finally, you see this screen:

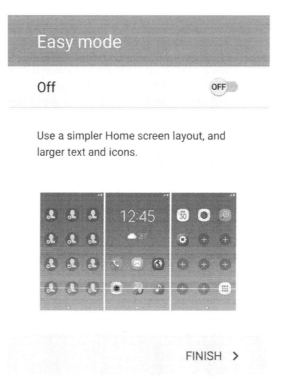

- Easy Mode simplifies your Galaxy's TouchWiz interface by stripping out the more advanced features.
- Skip it by tapping "Finish." With this book, you won't need Easy Mode. And if you do enable it, you'll find that things don't match up with the images and instructions in this book.

Welcome to the Home Screen

- Your Galaxy works for a few seconds and then brings you to a screen like this: the home screen.

- Tap "Later" to dismiss Samsung Smart Switch. If you followed the instructions throughout this chapter, you should have already transferred all data from your old phone. If, for some reason, there is still data on your old phone that wasn't transferred, Smart Switch can probably help you transfer it. Read more about Smart Switch here (p. 86).

- You may see a screen like the one below, indicating an operating system (OS) upgrade is available for your S7. If so, tap "Install Now" to update your phone. This process usually only takes 10-15 minutes and I recommend completing it right away.

- You'll be seeing a lot more of the home screen soon, but first, a few final steps.

Final Steps

- The initial setup process is finished, but there are a few more steps to take before using your Galaxy. If you're brand new to Android, feel free to come back to these steps after you've worked through the next chapter—but don't forget about them. They're important.

- First, configure your voicemail inbox. This is usually only necessary if you're a new customer to your carrier. To do so, tap the Phone app and tap  below the star ("*") key. Follow the voice prompts to set up your inbox for the first time.

- Second, set up device tracking (p. 208) through Google. With device tracking, you're able to geographically locate your Galaxy if it's lost or stolen. Although this is no guarantee of recovering your Galaxy, it gives you a much greater chance of doing so than if you don't have tracking enabled.

- Third, set up SOS messages (p. 260) so you can send an emergency message with a triple press of the power button. Hopefully you'll never need to use this feature, but it's better to have it enabled and not need it than vice-versa.

- Fourth, register your fingerprint in system settings (p. 63) → "Lock screen and security" → "Fingerprints." Your fingerprint is used to authenticate your identity for the lock screen, Samsung, Pay, and more.

- Last, claim your free offers (p. 237) from Samsung, if you qualify.

- With this all accomplished, you're ready to start learning more about your Galaxy.

Chapter 4: Fundamentals for New Users

Welcome to Android! More specifically, welcome to TouchWiz, Samsung's version of the Android user interface.

TouchWhat? Let me explain.

You probably already know that Google makes the Android OS. Android is an operating system like Microsoft Windows or Mac OSX, but it's designed for smartphones and tablets instead of desktops and laptops. However, Google's "pure" form of Android is only loaded on a few select devices such as Google's own Nexus series. Most Android devices come from third-party companies like Samsung that put their own software "layer" on top of the Android operating system. (That's a totally different product philosophy than Apple. Apple makes 100% of iPhones and iPads, and they all run exactly the same operating system with no additional "layers".)

TouchWiz is the layer that Samsung puts on top of Google's "pure" form of the Android OS. TouchWiz isn't just an app, though—it's a collection of apps, tweaks, features, and graphics. It refers to the entirety of the changes that Samsung makes to the Android OS to make it a unique Samsung experience. Vague, I know, but let me explain further.

To be more specific, some of TouchWiz's features include:

- A custom home screen (p. 64) and app drawer (p. 82);
- A custom system settings (p. 63) menu;
- Samsung apps like S Health (p. 243);
- A better camera (p. 123) app;
- A smattering of special features like Multi Window (p. 201);
- A custom app switcher (p. 60);
- And more.

Think of it this way: An HP computer runs the Windows OS but comes pre-loaded with HP-specific software layered on top of Windows. It's still a Windows computer but it's customized. TouchWiz refers to all the Samsung-specific stuff that's layered on top of Android. It's still the same Android operating system under the hood, but with Samsung's extra features and tweaks.

To demonstrate visually, here's an example of the TouchWiz home screen (first image) compared to the pure Android home screen (second image):

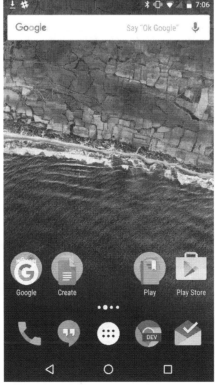

Different, but not *that* different, right? Right!

Parts of the User Interface

You can think about TouchWiz as six main parts:

- **System Settings**
- **The Home Screen(s)**
- **The Notification Panel**
- **The Lock Screen**
- **The App Drawer**
- **The App Switcher**

Almost everything you do on your Galaxy takes place in one of these areas, if not in an app itself. You can think of apps as your destinations and these parts of TouchWiz as the roads that get you to your destinations. In this chapter, I teach you everything there is to know about these areas of TouchWiz.

First, though, let's briefly talk about the physical controls on your Galaxy. You need to understand them before you can efficiently use your device.

Physical Controls – For the most basic operations

The Power Button (power on/off, restart, & emerg. mode)

- A single press of the power button wakes your Galaxy or puts it to sleep. I use the terms "wake" and "sleep" instead of "on" and "off" because your Galaxy is actually powered on even when it's asleep—it has to be, in order to receive calls and other communications.
- So how do you know whether you're waking it or putting it to sleep?
- If the screen is on, the device is awake. A single press of the power button puts it to sleep, and the screen turns off.
- When the screen is off, the device is asleep. A single press of the power button wakes it again and displays your lock screen (p. 81) (if enabled) to check that you're an authorized user.
- A triple press of the power button sends an SOS message (p. 260) to a specified contact, but only if you've set up SOS messages.
- A long press of the power button while the device is awake brings up the following options:

- **Power off:** Turn off the device completely. This is different than putting it to sleep with a single press of the power button. When powered off, it no longer sends or receives any communications at all. Turn the device on again with a long press of the power button.

- **Restart:** Reboot your Galaxy. Useful if it's exhibiting unusual or sluggish behavior. In fact, I recommend rebooting your Galaxy at least once every few days to keep it operating at its best. Try setting up Auto Restart (p. 255).

- **Emergency mode:** Enable a safety and power conservation mode called Emergency Mode (p. 260). Emergency Mode places big buttons on your home screen to easily share your location or use your camera's flash as a flashlight. Emergency mode also makes your battery last as long as possible by minimizing screen brightness, displaying only black and white, and slowing down the device's CPU. Useful if you're in a bad situation, if your battery is dying, or both.

Volume Up/Down Buttons (adjust volume, vibrate & silent modes)

> **TIP:** *Want your Galaxy to vibrate while it rings? Go to system settings → "Sounds and vibration" and enable "Vibrate while ringing."*

- Your Galaxy has five separate volume settings: Ringtone, Media, Notifications, System, and In-Call volume. This sounds complicated, but in practice you only have to remember one very simple rule: **The Volume Up and Volume Down buttons generally control what you want them to control, when you want it.**

- For example, if you're playing a game, they control the game's sound volume. If you're in a call, they control the speaker volume. When you're on the home screen, they control the ringtone volume. Easy, right?

- If you want the more complicated explanation, read on. Skip the rest of this section if you're not interested in the nuances of your Galaxy's volume controls.

Still with me? Okay. Here's what each volume setting controls, in detail:

- **Ringtone Volume:** The volume of the ringtone that plays when you receive a phone call.

- **Media Volume:** The volume of audio that plays in music apps, video apps, games, etc.

- **Notification Volume:** The volume of audio alerts that play upon receiving emails, text messages, and so on.

- **System Volume:** The volume of the phone keypad tone, touch sounds, key presses, and so on.

- **In-Call Volume:** The volume of the speaker when you're in a voice call.

- The Volume Up and Volume Down buttons only ever directly control Ringtone, Media, and In-Call volumes. Let me repeat that: The Volume buttons only ever directly adjust the Ringtone, Media, and In-Call volume levels, *not the notification or system volume levels*.

- Which setting is controlled depends on what the device is doing when you press the volume buttons. If your Galaxy is on a system screen such as a home screen or the app drawer, the buttons adjust the Ringtone volume. If it is playing a video or a game, the buttons adjust the Media volume. If you are in a call, the buttons adjust the In-Call volume.

- The exception is that they *indirectly* control Notification and System volume if you turn down the Ringtone volume to zero. When the Ringtone volume is muted,

Notification and System volumes are also temporarily muted. So, how do you specifically adjust the Notification and System volume levels, since the buttons don't control them? It's only possible with on-screen controls. Anytime you press Volume Up or Volume Down, tap the ⌄ icon to manually adjust these volume levels on the device, as shown below.

- Note that In-Call volume cannot be adjusted from this menu. It can only be adjusted while a voice call is active.
- Finally, **hold Volume Up or Volume Down** to rapidly increase or decrease the Ringtone or Media volume, but note that when holding Volume Down, the volume slider pauses at vibrate mode, which is still one notch above the mute setting. Release the Volume Down button and press it one more time to fully mute the device. (You can also mute the device by holding the power button and tapping "Mute" on the menu that appears.)
- If that all sounds complicated... well, that's because it is. Refer to this section if you get confused about the volume settings on your device, but fortunately, you'll find what I said earlier to be true: **The Volume Up and Volume Down buttons generally control what you want them to control, when you want it.**

Home Button (go to home screen, launch Camera, launch Now on Tap)

- The physical button centered below your Galaxy's screen is the home button ⬭.

- Pressing it once takes you back to the home screen (p. 64) from any other screen.

- Quickly double-pressing it opens the Camera (p. 123) (even when the device is asleep, which is extremely useful).

- Pressing and holding it opens Now on Tap (p. 181), a Google Now (p. 174) feature that I discuss in more depth later.

- The home button also doubles as the fingerprint scanner.

Recent and Back Buttons (App Switcher, Multi Window, go back)

- The recent (▱) and back (↩) buttons are soft buttons (i.e., non-click, touch buttons) to the left and right of ⬭, respectively, and are only visible when backlit.

- Tapping ▱ opens the App Switcher, a list of all of currently running apps. From here, swipe up and down with one finger to scroll through the list. Switch to an app by tapping it, or close an app by tapping ⊠ or by swiping it left or right. At the bottom of the screen is the "Close All" button, which terminates all currently running apps.

- It's not necessary to close apps to free up memory like on a computer. Android automatically manages memory, and you don't actually "quit" most apps—instead, you just hit ⬭ to "exit" them and they keep running in the background. The most common reason for completely quitting an app using the App Switcher is if it's acting buggy.

- Some apps have a ▤ button next to ⊠. This button launches the app in Multi Window (p. 201) mode.

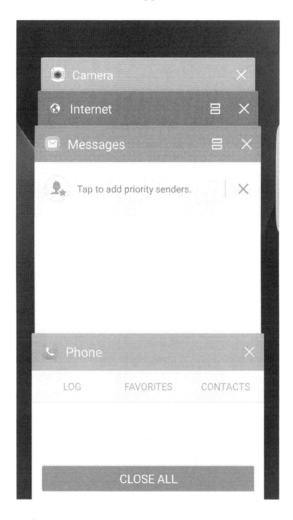

- The back button works similarly to a back button in a web browser, taking you to the last screen you were on. However, it sometimes does other things like hiding the on-screen keyboard or collapsing an open menu. The best way to get the hang of the back button is just to try it.

- If you've owned an Android device in the past, you may be wondering where the menu button is. The answer is that it's gone, completely replaced by the recent button. Instead, look for the on-screen "More" button to see menu options. (If you're upgrading from a Kit Kat device, note that "More" has replaced Kit Kat's three-dot ⋮ on-screen menu button.)

TIP: *You can also tap and hold the* ⤺ *button to open the menu on any screen.*

Basic Touch Screen Gestures

There are six basic touch screen gestures that are mentioned repeatedly throughout this book. Make sure you understand them:

- **Tapping:** A single tap of your finger. Commonly used to open apps, to press ⧉ or ↰ , to type on the keyboard, and to select menu items.
- **Tapping and holding:** A tap where your finger remains on the screen for at least half a second. Commonly used to access secondary options. Adjust the tap & hold delay in system settings → "Accessibility" → "Dexterity and interaction" → "Press and hold delay."
- **Tapping, holding, and dragging:** A tap where your finger remains on the screen for at least half a second, followed by movement without lifting your finger. Commonly used to move on-screen items.
- **Double-tapping:** A quick double-tap of your finger, where your finger completely lifts from the screen in between taps. Commonly used to zoom in and out of text in web browsers.
- **Swiping:** A fluid up, down, left, or right directional motion where your finger slides across the screen. Commonly used to scroll through menus, or page through different screens.
- **Pinching:** Using your thumb and index finger to pinch inwards or outwards. Commonly used to zoom in and out of text and photos.

System Settings – Very Important!

- You need to be **very familiar** with the system settings screen on your Galaxy, because I refer to it many times throughout this book. The system settings screen is the central control panel for your device. It includes settings for sounds, the display, wireless connections, power conservation, and much more.

- System settings are accessed in two ways. Either tap the "Settings" app in your app drawer (p. 82) or swipe down the notification panel (p. 75) and tap ✿.

- Any time you're having trouble finding something in the system settings, use the "Search" feature.

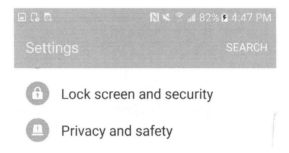

Resetting System Settings

- Android 6.0 Marshmallow has a new feature to reset all your system settings to default, in case you make a change you can't figure out how to undo. This feature only affects system settings, not user apps or app data.

- To use it, go to system settings → "Backup and reset" → "Reset settings."

The Home Screen – Where the action starts

- Now that you're familiar with the basic controls of your Galaxy, we can discuss its software.
- If you still have this screen pulled up, then you're on the home screen.

- If you don't see this screen, just press ⬭ and you're taken to it. Your home screen may look slightly different depending on your carrier and to what degree you've already customized your device.

What's the Home Screen?

- The home screen is where everything starts on Android; you might compare it to the desktop of your computer.
- Unlike on a computer, none of the icons on the Android home screen are files. Instead, they're all shortcuts to apps. You may be used to saving files on the desktop

of your computer, but that's not possible on Android. Files can only be accessed from *within* apps and mostly stay behind the scenes.

- Android has multiple home screens, not just a single desktop like most computers.
- From the home screen, try swiping left and right. This accesses secondary, adjacent home screens on which you can put additional app shortcuts and widgets. Swiping all the way left opens Briefing (p. 288), a news and social media aggregator. Briefing is technically an app, not a part of the home screen, but Briefing's developers have entered into an agreement with Samsung to prominently feature it. I recommend disabling (p. 249) Briefing.

Components of the Home Screen

- There are many things happening on the home screen, so let's analyze them from top to bottom.
- In the following image, I have outlined the seven major parts of the default home screen.

- The horizontal bar at the very top of the screen is called the **status bar**. From right to left it contains the current time, the battery/charging status, the cell signal strength, the Wi-Fi signal strength, the ringtone mute indicator, and the NFC status.

- The two icons in the left corner of the status bar are notifications (p. 75). Don't worry about these yet—I explain them in more detail later in this section.

- Below the status bar is a widget (p. 68) displaying the current weather conditions (though, this one hasn't been configured yet).

- Widgets can be nearly any size and contain a variety of different content. In essence, they are mini "apps" that you place on your home screen for easy, bite-size functionality and information. More info on widgets is coming up shortly.

- The Google box below the time/weather widget is also a widget. This widget allows you to quickly perform a Google web or voice search.

- Below the two widgets is a row of **app shortcuts**, including Email, Camera, Play Store, and a folder full of Google apps.

- These aren't widgets; rather, they're shortcuts that you tap to open apps. Samsung has placed these four app shortcuts on the home screen by default, but I'll show you how to customize them shortly.

- The next element is a row of symbols that includes a ⌂.

- In this screenshot, the ⌂ is solid white, indicating that the device is currently showing the **main home screen**.

- Each of the ● icons represent a **secondary home screen**. Switch to these secondary home screens by swiping left or right.

- The  to the left of the house represents <u>Briefing</u> (p. 288).

- Below is an example of a secondary home screen, accessed by swiping right from the main home screen.
- It's not fundamentally different than the main home screen; it just provides additional space for more app shortcuts and widgets.
- As you can see, this one has been preconfigured with several app shortcuts and a Galaxy Essentials widget.
- Notice that one of the ⬜ icons is now solid white instead of ⌂, indicating that it's a secondary home screen.

⭐ **TIP:** *From nearly any screen on your Galaxy, press* ⬭ *to return to the last home screen you were viewing. If it was a secondary home screen, press* ⬭ *again to return to the main home screen.*

- The bottommost element of the home screen is the **app tray**.
- The app tray is a special place for you to place your most important app shortcuts, and unlike other app shortcuts, these stay visible on all home screens.
- By default, the app tray contains Phone, Contacts, Messages, Internet, and Apps (a special shortcut to the app drawer (p. 82) that can't be removed).

⭐ **TIP:** *As you may have noticed, the shortcuts in the app tray stay the same regardless of which home screen you're viewing, unlike the app shortcuts on the home screens themselves. This is why the app tray is a great place to put your most-used apps.*

- Finally, on the right-hand edge of the screen is the Edge Tab, if you have an S7 Edge.
- Read more about Edge features in Chapter 6 (p. 188).

What Are Widgets?

You've now seen a few different widgets on the home screen—the weather widget, the Google search widget, and the Galaxy Essentials widget. Let's define "widget" a little better.

Widgets are mini-apps that live right on your home screen. Unlike full apps, which typically have a lot of features and options and occupy the entire screen, widgets are designed to do only one or two high-priority things right from your home screen.

For example, consider the time/date/weather widget that's on the main home screen by default. Without it, you'd have to open a web browser and do Google searches to get the same information—much more difficult than a simple glance at your main home screen. The time/date/weather widget is all about providing convenient access to time/date/weather information.

Simply put, widgets give you easier and faster access to information or tasks that you might need on a regular basis so you don't have to open an app every time. There are thousands of widgets available for download from the Google Play Store (p. 166), and you can find a widget for nearly anything. For example, there are stock tickers, news headlines, smart appliance controls, and so on. Also, many full apps come with widgets to provide convenient access to commonly used features.

Editing Existing Shortcuts and Widgets

- The strength of the home screen is its customizability, so let's talk about how to make your home screen your own by customizing your shortcuts and widgets.
- We'll start with the default home screen:

- Let's say I want to rearrange the Email, Camera, Play Store, and Google folder shortcuts.

- Normally, this is very simple: just **tap and hold** on the shortcuts one at a time, **drag** them to their new locations, and **release**:

- However, let's say I want to put them along the top of the screen, so there's a bit of a problem—the weather widget is in the way.

- It turns out that, as with app shortcuts, tapping, holding, and dragging is also the way to manipulate widgets.

- So, I tap and hold the weather widget, drag it up to the "Remove" icon that appears, and release it.

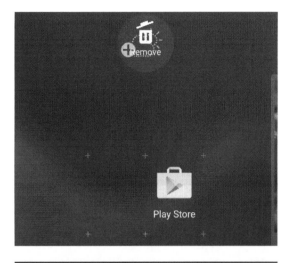

- This is much better. Now, there's room for the app shortcuts at the top of the screen.
- I tap and hold each of these shortcuts for approximately a second, drag, and release.

- By tapping, holding, and dragging, I have rearranged the row of app shortcuts as shown above.

> ⭐ **TIP:** *Manipulate app shortcuts in the <u>app tray</u> (p. 68) at the bottom of the screen in the same way—just tap, hold, and drag. Note that dragging an app shortcut over an existing app shortcut in the app tray automatically creates a new folder in the app tray containing both app shortcuts. To replace an app in the app tray, remove one before you add one.*

- To resize a widget, tap and hold it until you see a blue outline. Then, tap and drag the blue dots.

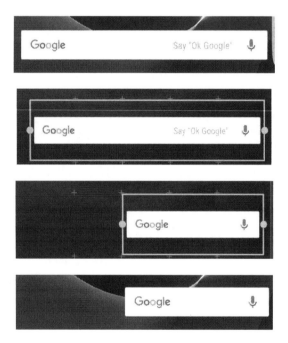

- Tap ⮌ to confirm your changes.
- Move app shortcuts and widgets to secondary home screens by tapping, dragging, and holding them against the left or right edge of the screen.

Adding Widgets, Changing Wallpaper & Theme, & Managing Home Screens

- To add widgets (p. 68), change your background image, change your theme, or edit/add/delete secondary home screens, you need to pull up the **home screen menu**.

- Do so by tapping and holding any blank space on the home screen.

From this menu, you can:

- **Add, rearrange or remove home screens:** Swipe left and right to view and edit your currently active home screens. To remove a home screen and all of its app shortcuts and widgets, tap and hold until you feel a vibration, drag it up to the "Remove" icon, and release. To rearrange home screens, tap, hold, and drag them to the left or right sides of the screen. To add a new home screen, swipe all the way to the right and tap the plus (+) sign. You can create an unlimited number of secondary home screens, although I find that it's rarely practical to have more than five or six.

- **Change wallpaper:** Your wallpaper is the background image shown on the home screen and/or lock screen (p. 81). Tap the "Wallpapers" icon to select from a variety of other preloaded options. To use a photo taken with your device's camera instead, after you've tapped "Wallpapers," tap the "From Gallery" button in the lower-left-hand corner of the screen. When on the wallpaper selection screen, tap the down arrow next to "Home screen" to specify whether the selected wallpaper should be applied to the home screen only, the home and lock screens, or the lock screen only. Note that using darker wallpaper increases your battery life (p. 284).

- **Add widgets:** To view all the widgets available on your device and optionally add them to a home screen, tap the "Widgets" button. From this screen, swipe left and right to scroll through all available widgets. Once you've found a widget you want to place on one of your home screens, tap and hold until you feel a vibration. Drag and hold your finger over the far left or right side of the screen to switch between home screens. When you've found a place for your widget, release your finger. Note that some third-party apps come with widgets, which automatically appear in this Widgets repository when the apps themselves are installed.

- **Change theme:** Theming is a new TouchWiz feature that lets you totally change the look of your Galaxy. Themes not only include wallpaper, but also replacement icons and system sounds. Tap "Themes" to download and activate themes from the Samsung store. You need to be logged into your Samsung account (p. 48) to download themes.

- **Change the screen grid:** Tap "Screen grid" to change the number of app rows and columns. Choose from 4x4, 4x5, and 5x5.

TIP: Wondering how to add new app shortcuts to the home screen, instead of just moving around existing ones? Keep reading— it's coming up in the section about the app drawer (p. 82).

The Notification Panel – System settings & get important info

- Congratulations—you've learned almost everything you need to know about home screens on TouchWiz.

- Now, I'll discuss the **notification panel**, which is another very important component of your Galaxy's user interface.

- Place your finger on the status bar—the bar at the very top of your device's screen containing the time—and swipe down. You see a screen like this:

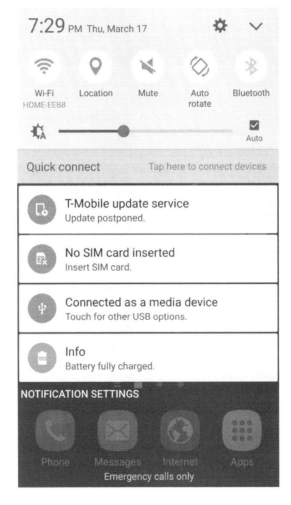

- This is the notification panel.

- Whereas the home screen(s) are dedicated to widgets and app shortcuts, the notification panel is a place where your device reports important status information and provides quick access to some commonly used settings.

- Let's break down the parts of the notification panel the same way we did for the home screen.

Components of the Notification Panel

- At the top of the screen are the current time and date as well as two buttons— 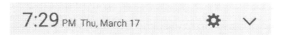 and ∨.

- Tapping ✿ takes you to system settings, which is the same as accessing the "Settings" app in the <u>app drawer</u> (p. 82).
- Tapping ∨ expands the group of **toggle buttons** that include Wi-Fi, Location, Sound, Auto Rotate, and Bluetooth. Each of these buttons is called a toggle button because it either switches a simple setting on or off, or rotates through a group of settings. For example, the Wi-Fi toggle button turns your Wi-Fi connection on or off. The Sound toggle button changes your sound settings from "Sound" (all sounds on), to "Vibrate" (sounds off; vibration on), to "Mute" (all sounds & vibration off).

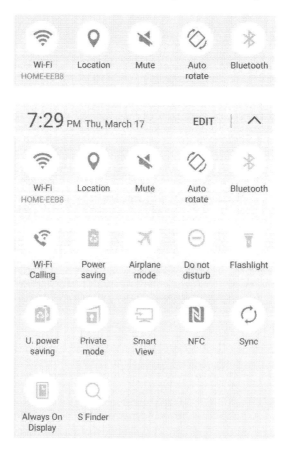

TIP: *Tap and hold any of these notification toggles to open their corresponding settings page.*

- Tapping "Edit" switches to a mode in which you tap, hold, and drag toggle buttons to rearrange them.
- Tap "Done" when you've achieved your desired arrangement.

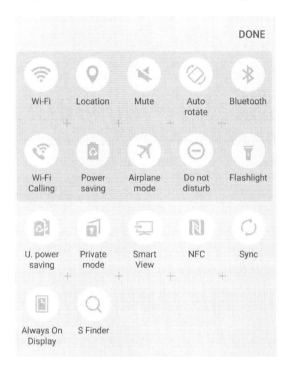

- Notice how only 5 icons are shown by in the toggle button cluster by default, yet 10 total icons are shown in the shaded area above.
- How do you access icons 6-10? By swiping the main group of toggle buttons left and right to gain access to the second row of toggle buttons from the expanded view.
- For example, here I have swiped the toggle buttons partway to the left:

- This swiping action doesn't access any of the additional toggle buttons in the third or fourth row of the expanded view—only the first two rows.

- Below the toggle buttons are the screen brightness selector and the <u>Quick Connect</u> (p. 235) button.

- Checking the "Auto" box makes your device automatically adjust the brightness of the screen by measuring the ambient light level.

- Control the brightness manually by moving the slider.

- Below this is the main notification area.

- In this area, you find notifications from apps or from the Android OS itself.

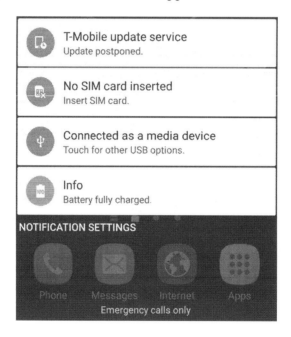

Working with Notifications

- **Notifications** are the means by which apps communicate with you when they're in the background.

- Notifications are very important because they let your device perform valuable services behind the scenes without your direct attention.

- For example, by default your Galaxy's Messages app sends you a notification every time you receive a text message. Other apps like stock tickers send you alerts whenever required, such as when a stock hits a target price.

- In the following screenshot, the Gmail app has notified me of a new email:

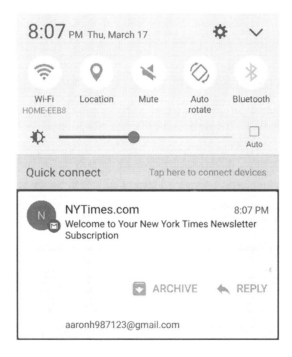

- Here, tap "Reply" to start composing a reply in the Gmail app, or "Archive" to remove the email from the inbox.

- Tapping the notification opens the email.

- Most notifications do something when you tap them, even if they don't have mini action buttons like "Reply" and "Archive." For example, you receive a notification every time you install a new app from the Google Play Store (p. 166). You won't see an "Open" button, but tapping the notification opens the app. So, any time you want to follow up on a notification but it doesn't have mini-buttons, just try tapping it.

- Notifications generally disappear ("are dismissed") after you tap them. Or, tap the "Clear" button to dismiss all notifications without tapping them individually and triggering their actions. For example, tapping "Clear" on the screen above dismisses the email notification without opening the Gmail app.

- To clear a single notification without tapping it, swipe it left or right.

TIP: You can expand and contract some notifications by placing two fingers on them and dragging up/down. For example, do this with Gmail notifications to show and hide the "Reply" and "Archive" buttons, or with text message notifications to show and hide "Call" and "Reply" buttons.

- Some notifications are persistent and cannot be cleared.
- For example, my carrier offers Wi-Fi calling and my S7 displays a persistent notification whenever it's enabled. In this case, hitting "Clear" does not remove that notification, and tapping it does nothing. A USB connection notification is another example of a persistent notification.
- That's everything you need to know about the notification panel. You'll find it's a very important part of your user experience.
- To close the notification panel, either swipe up from the bottom of the screen or tap ⤺ .

TIP: On some screens the status bar at the top of the screen is hidden. Swipe down once from the top of the screen to reveal it, and then again to open the notification panel.

The Lock Screen – Protect your personal information

- The security risk involved in owning an Android smartphone is higher than ever because they contain so much more sensitive data than 'dumb' phones. In the past, cellphones contained only your phone book and perhaps some text messages; today, they contain your e-mail, photos, your banking information, your passwords, and so on.

- The lock screen is the main security mechanism to protect your data. When active, the lock screen prevents your device from being used unless you provide the appropriate authentication.

- Typically, the lock screen is activated every time the device goes to sleep and a password is required every time it is woken up.

- The screenshot below shows the lock screen with the PIN function enabled:

- Instead of a PIN, it's possible to use fingerprint recognition (my recommendation), pattern recognition, or a password.

- It's also possible to disable the lock screen entirely or to use a zero-security, swipe-to-unlock option, but if you value your personal information at all, I don't suggest using these options.

- In addition to securing your phone, the lock screen conveniently shows notifications from your apps:

- Tap any notification once before unlocking your device, and you're be taken to its respective app immediately when your device unlocks, just like tapping a notification in the notification panel.

- Or, swipe a notification left or right to dismiss it from the lock screen.

- You'll learn more about setting up your lock screen (p. 206) shortly. For now, I just want you to understand what it's for and how it works.

The App Drawer – View all apps, delete apps, & create app shortcuts

- Another important part of TouchWiz is the **app drawer**.

- It contains all the apps installed on your Galaxy, including those preloaded on your Galaxy as well as any third-party apps you've installed from the Google Play Store (p. 166) or other sources.

- To open the app drawer, tap the "Apps" shortcut in the app tray:

- Upon doing so, you see a screen like this:

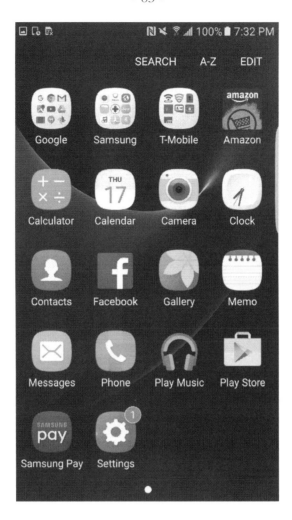

- This is the **app drawer** and it contains shortcuts to *all* the apps installed on your Galaxy, unlike the home screens, where you selectively place the shortcuts (and widgets) you want. In other words, the app drawer is a complete directory of installed apps.

- By now, much of this screen should look familiar. At the top of the screen is the same status bar that's on the home screen and you can still swipe it down to reveal the notification panel (p. 75). The lion's share of the screen is covered by app shortcuts, which launch apps just like they do on the home screen. At the bottom of the screen is a small circle, indicating there is only one page of apps. Multiple circles would indicate you could swipe left and right to access additional screens. There is no 'main' screen in the app drawer like there is with the home screens.

- There are three buttons in the app drawer not found on the home screen: "Search", "A-Z," and "Edit."

- "Search" lets you search the names of installed apps to find the app you want to open.

- "A-Z" alphabetizes the apps in your app drawer. This is useful to "reset" your app drawer if you've rearranged apps using "Edit" or if you've installed new apps, which by default are added at the end of your app drawer.
- "Edit" lets you:
  - o **Organize apps in your app drawer:** To rearrange apps, tap and hold until you feel a vibration, then drag the app to its desired location and release. Note that to place an app between two other apps, you must hold it for an additional ~1 second *in between* the icons until they shift position and make room for the app you're moving. Holding the app directly over another app instead of next to it creates a new folder instead of moving the app.
  - o **Create a new folder to organize your apps:** To create a new folder with two or more apps, tap and hold an app until you feel a vibration, then drag the app directly over another app until you see a white border appear. Then release. A new folder is created containing both apps. Move additional apps into this folder using the same tap, hold, and drag method.
  - o **Remove a folder:** To remove an existing folder, tap it and then tap "Delete folder." This does not delete apps inside the folder—it just returns them to the app drawer.
  - o **Delete or disable apps:** Tap to completely uninstall downloaded apps or disable non-essential apps (p. 252) that come preloaded on the device. Samsung doesn't allow you to completely uninstall preloaded apps, but disabling them freezes them and prevents them from running. I recommend disabling any built-in apps you don't use, because it frees up memory, improves system performance, and increases battery life. In particular, feel free to disable carrier "bloatware"—any apps preloaded on your Galaxy that you know you'll never use. (I'm looking at you, "Samsung Milk Music.") To re-enable any disabled apps, go to system settings → "Applications" → "Application manager" → "All apps" → "Disabled".
- To exit Edit mode, tap or "Done."

Adding New App Shortcuts to Your Home Screen

- When you tap and hold an app shortcut in the app drawer (p. 82), your Galaxy displays a silhouette of your home screens and gives you a chance to copy the shortcut to one of your home screens (p. 64) or the app tray (p. 68) if it has a free slot.
- Below, I have tapped and held the Amazon app in the app drawer, and my Galaxy is directing me to place a shortcut on my main home screen. To do so, I would simply position the Amazon shortcut where I want it and release.

- Had I wanted to place the shortcut on a secondary home screen, I would have dragged the shortcut to the far left or right edge of the screen, held it until the home screen switched over, and then released it.

- As you may recall, this action is different than tapping and holding an existing app shortcut that's already on a home screen—in that case, tapping and holding lets you move the shortcut around on your home screens, remove it altogether, or place it into a folder.

To summarize:

- **Tapping and holding apps in the app drawer creates *new* shortcuts on your home screen (p. 64) or in the app tray (p. 68).**

- **Tapping and holding existing app shortcuts that are already on your home screen lets you edit or move them.**

- **The app drawer is a complete app directory; home screens are for your most-used apps and widgets only.**

Transferring Your Data from Another Phone

By now, you should be getting comfortable with your Galaxy. You've seen all the major parts of the user interface and you're getting a sense of how they all work together. But there's another important topic to cover before we move on—what's the best way to transfer data from your previous phone? You may already have transferred your data using the tools available during initial device setup (see Chapter 3 (p. 24)), but if not, here are your options.

From an Android That Supports NFC—Use Tap & Go

If you're switching from an Android device that supports NFC wireless communication, you can use the Android "Tap & Go" feature to transfer your Google account, apps, app data, Wi-Fi passwords, and system settings.

A couple caveats:

- Tap & Go is only available when you first set up your device. To use Tap & Go after setting up your device, you have to perform a factory reset (p. 260) to completely wipe your device and start from scratch as described in Chapter 3 (p. 24).
- Tap & Go doesn't transfer your SMS/MMS messages or Gallery photos. To transfer these, use Samsung Smart Switch as described below, *after* using Tap & Go.

Not sure if your previous Android device supports NFC? As long as it was made in the last 3-4 years, it probably does. But to be sure, consult its instruction manual or search Google.

From a non-NFC Android, iPhone, or BlackBerry—Samsung Smart Switch

If you can't or don't want to use Tap & Go, the next best option is Samsung's exclusive Smart Switch program. Samsung realized that its customers wanted an easy and fast way to transfer data to their new phones and created a good, reliable program to do just that.

It runs on both Windows and Mac OS, and allows you to transfer your data from almost any iPhone, Android, BlackBerry, or Symbian phone. In fact, if you're switching from another Android smartphone or from an iPhone and you have an iCloud account, you don't need to install any desktop software at all—only the Smart Switch mobile app, available from the Google Play Store (p. 166) and Apple App Store.

Smart Switch also makes it easy to transfer photos and text messages. It complements Tap & Go nicely, since Tap & Go doesn't copy these things.

Whatever your situation is, the Smart Switch website has clear, step-by-step instructions. Start here:

http://www.samsung.com/us/smart-switch/

From a Dumb Phone

If your new Galaxy is your first smartphone and your last phone was a "dumb" phone, there's good and bad news. The good news is that you won't have much information to transfer—probably just phone numbers. The bad news is that data transfer programs are becoming less common as dumb phones are becoming less common. Your luck will depend on what make and model your last phone was.

Because there are hundreds, if not thousands of dumb phone models in existence, I can't offer you a one-size-fits-all solution. However, I can offer you some general advice. Here are the steps you should take to get your contacts from your dumb phone to your Galaxy:

1. First, take both phones to one of your carrier's retail stores and ask if they can help. These stores usually have special, industrial devices that can transfer your data. This is the easiest and cheapest option in most cases.
2. If the store's transfer device isn't compatible with your old phone, you can try to save your contacts to your SIM card using your dumb phone and then import them to your Galaxy. This only works if your dumb phone has a contact export feature (so consult its instruction manual), and also uses a nano-SIM card like your Galaxy (many older phones used micro- or mini-SIM cards; in that case, this method won't work). If, after consulting your old phone's instruction manual, you are able to export your contacts to your nano-SIM card, pop it back into your Galaxy and go to Contacts → "More" → "Settings" → "Import/Export contacts" → "Import" → "SIM card." Save the contacts to your Google account.
3. If these methods fail to accomplish what you need, it's time to start Googling. Search Google for **(make and model of your old phone) transferring contacts to android**. With any luck, you'll find a solution for to your particular situation. Some of them may require purchasing software or computer cables.
4. Failing that, sit down, get comfortable, and manually enter phone numbers into your Contacts (p. 138) app the old-fashioned way. Sorry!

If your old dumb phone has other data you want to transfer, like photos or MP3 files, your best bet is to consult the phone's instruction manual to learn how to copy those files to an SD memory card. From there, you can copy those files to your computer, and then onto your Galaxy using the USB file transfer techniques in Chapter 8 (p. 272).

Chapter 5: Basic Functions

So far, you've learned the basics of TouchWiz, including the home screen, the notification panel, the lock screen, the app drawer, and more. Now, I show you how to perform basic functions such as making phone calls, sending text messages, browsing the Internet, taking pictures and video, and more.

Landscape Mode

- Landscape Mode works in almost all apps—but not on the home screen, app drawer, notification panel, or lock screen. When you're in an app, just flip your Galaxy sideways and it automatically enters landscape mode.

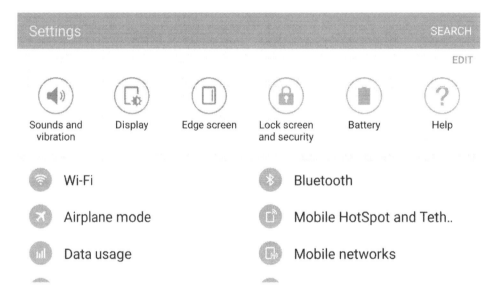

- If your Galaxy doesn't enter landscape mode when you flip it sideways, swipe down the notification panel and make sure the Screen Rotation toggle button is set to "Auto rotate."
- You can also use this toggle button to lock the display to Portrait mode if you don't want your screen to automatically rotate.

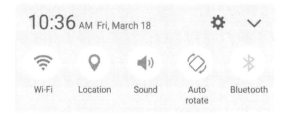

Entering Text

Inputting text is one of the most basic functions you need to know. There are several ways to do so:

- Typing with the on-screen keyboard;
- Swiping with the on-screen keyboard, and;
- Dictating by voice.

Typing with the On-Screen Keyboard

- The default input method is the on-screen Samsung keyboard. It looks like this:

- In my opinion, the Samsung keyboard is excellent. It allows both tapping and swiping (discussed below), has well-placed punctuation keys, and includes a number row that's accessible without tapping a modifier key first. I always use the Samsung keyboard.
- However, the Samsung keyboard is only one of many keyboards available for Android devices. Other keyboards can be downloaded and installed from the Google Play Store, and each one looks and works a little differently. For example, the official Google keyboard has a more minimalist look and sacrifices the number row for larger letter keys:

TIP: If the Samsung keyboard isn't for you, try other options from the Google Play Store like the Google Keyboard shown above, SwiftKey, or Swype.

Here's what you need to know about using the Samsung keyboard:

- Tap shift ( ) to cycle through lowercase, initial uppercase, and caps lock.
- Tap and hold any character key to access accented and other secondary characters.
- Tap "Sym" to switch between the standard keyboard and symbols.
- As you type, your Galaxy predicts words in the gray bar above the keyboard. Tap any word to autocomplete the word you are typing. This saves a lot of time. Tap to save a new word into the dictionary, or tap to see more autocomplete options.
- Tap once to activate voice input (discussed below), or tap and hold it to access keyboard settings:

From left to right, these settings include:

- : Activate Voice Input (p. 92) (same as tapping once)
- : Show Recent Clipboard Items
- : Show Emoji (emoticons).

- ⚙: Samsung Keyboard Settings (same as going to system settings→ "Language and input" → "Samsung keyboard")

There are many settings available for the Samsung keyboard such as auto-prediction, auto-punctuation, sound and vibration, and more. One particularly useful setting is Text Shortcuts (p. 255), which let you specify abbreviations that your Galaxy automatically expands. For example, Text Shortcuts can expand "sth" into "something," or "bc" into "because."

Swiping for Speedy Input

- In 2010, a small software developer released a keyboard called Swype. Swype was the first Android keyboard to offer typing by swiping. With this type of input, instead of tapping letters one at a time, you place your finger on the first character of the word you want and trace from letter to letter without tapping at all.

- Once I tried Swype, I never looked back – as did millions of other Android users. Today, you can still download Swype from the Google Play Store, but you don't need to because Samsung includes the same functionality in the Samsung keyboard.

- I strongly suggest you learn to type by swiping, as it's much faster and easier than tapping. It also considerably reduces thumb strain.

- Below is a screenshot of me swiping the word "Hello." You can see the path of my finger over the keys.

⭐ **TIP:** *On the S7 and S7 Edge you can type multiple words by swiping, without lifting your finger at all. Simply move your finger over the spacebar in between words.*

Dictating Text Using Voice Recognition

- Dictation is another way to input text. To activate voice input mode, tap on a text input field to bring up the Samsung keyboard, and then tap 🎤 once. You can begin speaking as soon as the following screen appears:

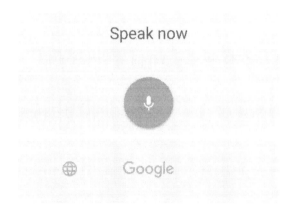

- Tap 🎤 to pause dictation or tap ⊕ to change languages.
- Voice recognition is surprisingly accurate and Google is improving it all the time. In particular, I find it very handy when I have to use my phone while driving. I suggest you give voice recognition input a shot, because it's the real deal—not a gimmick like voice recognition technology was a few years ago.

Copy and Paste

- TouchWiz makes it easy to copy and paste text.
- First, select text. Tap and hold text in apps such as Messages, Gmail, any Internet browser, and so on:

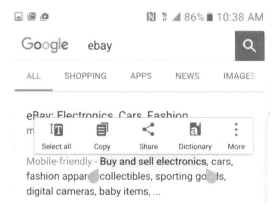

- Move the blue tabs around to select text, and then tap "Copy."

- In some apps, there's a slightly different copy/paste toolbar, but it works the same way:

- After you've copied your text, tap and hold the text field you want to paste into, and then tap "Paste."
- Alternatively, to access data that you previously copied, tap "Clipboard" and then the content you want to paste.

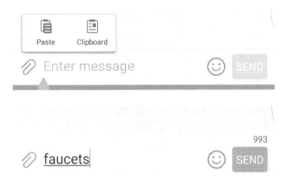

- Some apps have the following paste button instead, but it works the same way:

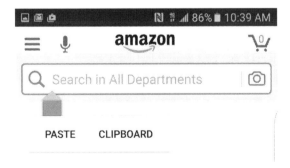

Airplane Mode

- Airplane mode leaves your device powered on, but turns off all wireless communications including cellular, Wi-Fi, Bluetooth, and NFC.
- Although use of electronic devices is now permitted from boarding to de-boarding on all U.S. airlines, you are still required to use airplane mode during takeoff and landing.
- Activate it by swiping the notification panel down with two fingers and tapping the "Airplane mode" toggle.

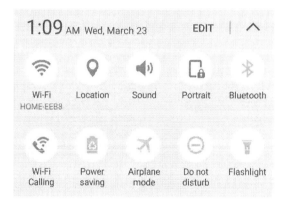

The Share Via Tool

- The Share Via tool appears in nearly every app. It's essential to the Android OS, and you need to understand how it works. The Share Via icon looks like this:

- Alternatively, in some apps it simply appears as a "Share" button:

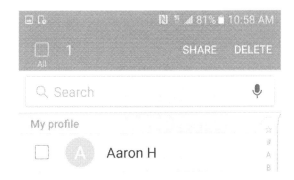

- Tapping the Share Via icon/button lets you **send content from one app to another, in order to take some action on it**.

- For example, you might want to send a photo from your Gallery app to a photo editing app, or to the Gmail app to send it as an email attachment. Or, you might want to send a document from the Microsoft Word app to a cloud storage app such as Dropbox. The Share Via tool is the means by which you send files from app to app.

- Let's see it in action. In the following screenshot I have tapped 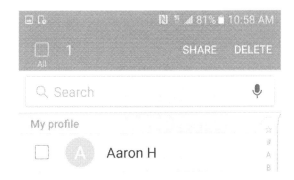 while viewing a photo in the Gallery app:

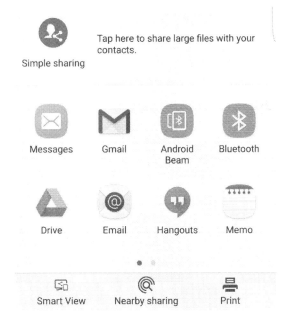

- Swipe left and right to see more options on the Share Via screen.

Using the Share Via tool, you can:

- Send the file to the Messages app, to send it as a MMS message;
- Send the file to Gmail, to send it as an email attachment;

- Send the file to Google Drive to upload it to cloud storage;
- Send it to another Android device with <u>Android Beam</u> (p. 212)
- Print it;
- and so on.

> **TIP:** *"Simple sharing" uploads your content to a Samsung website and then sends a link to the person you shared it with. In my opinion, "Simple sharing" is an unnecessary middle step. Skip "Simple sharing" and share files as email attachments instead, using the Gmail app.*

- As I mentioned, you'll see this tool all over your Galaxy. Its purpose is always the same: to send content from one app to another. It's kind of like a replacement for files and folders on a desktop computer. For example, if you want to email an attachment on a desktop computer, you'd click "Attach" and then browse your hard drive to find the desired file. On Android, files and folders are all hidden behind the scenes. Instead, you'd just open the desired file in its respective app (e.g., Gallery for photos) and then use the Share Via tool to send it to the Gmail app for use as an attachment.
- The bottom line is, **if you need to get a file from one app to another, look for the Share Via tool.**

Connecting to a Wi-Fi Network

- Need to connect to a wireless network at home, in an airport, in a coffee shop, etc.? Make sure the Wi-Fi toggle button is enabled in the notification panel and go to system settings → "Wi-Fi." You see a list of available networks:

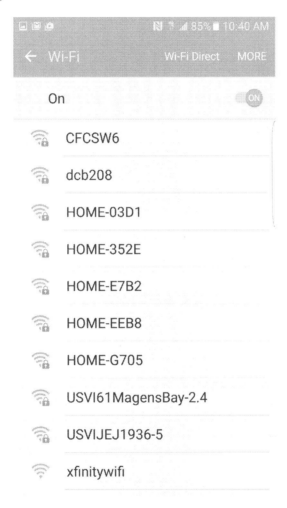

- Tap any network and follow the prompts to connect. If the network is secured, you're asked to enter a WEP/WPA password first.
- Alternatively, to connect to a router using WPS technology, press the WPS button ( ) on your router. Then, on your Galaxy tap "More" → "WPS push button." If your router supports WPS, this method lets you connect to the network without typing a password. Most modern routers support WPS and I personally like to use it when possible.
- If your network doesn't appear in the list, try toggling Wi-Fi off and on again and/or power-cycling your router.

TIP: *For some commercial Wi-Fi hotspots, such as the ones at Starbucks, you're able to connect to the network without a password, but after you're connected you need to open your browser and accept terms & conditions before you actually get Internet access. You usually receive a notification in your notification panel that you need to log in, but not always. So, if you connect to a public Wi-Fi hotspot but data isn't working, open your browser and try to load a web page. You should be redirected to a login page, and after logging in, you have Internet access.*

Browsing the Internet

- The S7 and S7 Edge come pre-loaded with two Internet browsers.
- The first is simply titled "Internet," and the second is the mobile version of Google Chrome.
- Although the stock Internet browser is not a bad browser, my suggestion is to skip it and go straight to Chrome—*especially* if you use Chrome on your desktop computer. Chrome is updated more often, is faster, and integrates with your Google account to automatically sync your desktop bookmarks, saved passwords, history, browser tabs, and more.
- Chrome is in your app drawer, inside the "Google" folder:

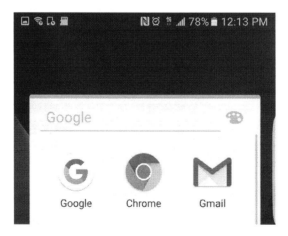

- Upon opening Chrome for the first time, accept Google's Terms of Service to continue and proceed to sign in with your Google account. When finished, you see the Google homepage:

- Enter web addresses (.com's, etc.) in the search box at the top of the screen, or simply enter keywords to search Google.
- Double-tap paragraphs to auto-fit webpages to the screen, or pinch with two fingers to zoom manually.
- Tap and hold text to copy and paste it (p. 92), or tap and hold links to bring up additional options.
- To view open tabs, tap ⬚ and they'll be listed alongside your currently running apps.
- Swipe left/right on the URL bar to go to the previous/next tab.
- Tap ⋮ to see the menu, where you can access other options including:
  - Open a new tab;
  - Open a new incognito tab (p. 101);
  - Access bookmarks;
  - View browsing history;
  - Share the current tab with the Share Via (p. 94) tool;

- o Print (p. 248) the current tab;
- o and more.

TIP: *Auto-fit and pinch-to-zoom usually only work when you're viewing desktop sites in mobile Chrome. If you're viewing a mobile-optimized site, often you'll find that zooming doesn't work. If this is a problem, you can force all websites to allow zooming. Tap* ⋮ → *"Settings" → "Accessibility" and check "Force enable zoom." From this screen you can also change the default text size to make websites easier to read on the device's screen.*

Tabbed Browsing

- By default, Chrome tabs are shown in the App Switcher (p. 60) alongside your currently running apps. To see them, tap ⬜.

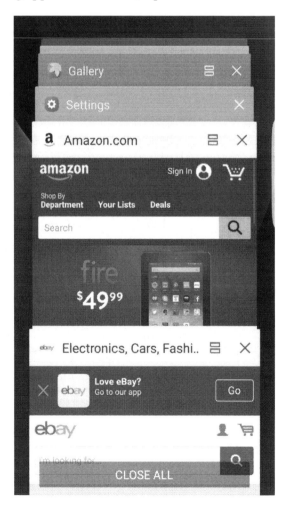

- Tap a tab to make it full screen.

> ⭐ **TIP:** *To separate your tabs from your currently running apps, go to* ⁝ *→ "Settings" → "Merge tabs and apps" and turn the slider off. Now, your tabs are accessible through the window switcher icon (* ③ *) next to* ⁝ *:*

Adding and Viewing Bookmarks

- To bookmark an open web page, tap ⁝ → ☆.
- To manage your bookmarks, tap ⁝ → "Bookmarks."
- Tap on folders to open them, and tap ⤺ to go to the previous folder.
- To edit, rename, delete, or move individual bookmarks, tap the ⁝ icon next to them.
- Unfortunately, there is no way to edit or delete folders using Chrome on your Android—you have to use the Bookmark Manager in a desktop version of Chrome that's logged into your Google account.

> ⭐ **TIP:** *If you add, remove, or edit bookmarks in the desktop version of Chrome, the changes are automatically synced to mobile Chrome, usually within 5-10 minutes. You don't need to take a manual action to synchronize the two browsers. The same principle holds true for other data that Chrome syncs, such as saved passwords, history, open tabs, and more.*

Private Browsing with Incognito Mode

- Sometimes, you might want to browse without leaving a trace in your browser history. No judgment.
- To do so, tap ⁝ → "New incognito tab." This new tab, which has a black background, lets you browse without recording your history, cookies, or any other record of the web pages you visit.

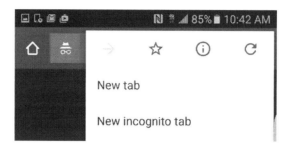

Viewing Open Tabs on Your Desktop Computer

- As long as your desktop Google Chrome is set to synchronize open tabs (in desktop Chrome settings → "Advanced Sync Settings"), you can access your currently open desktop tabs using your Galaxy.

- To do so, tap ⋮ → "Recent tabs." You see a list of devices synced with your Google account—look for your desktop computer and tap the tab you want to open on your Galaxy.

- This is a very convenient way to pick up where you left off on your desktop computer while on the go.

Overriding Mobile Web Themes

- While some websites have great mobile versions, others are just detestable, broken wastelands or are missing critical features. Not all businesses are up to date with their mobile websites.

- If this happens, try overriding the website's mobile theme by tapping ⋮ → "Request desktop site." This doesn't always work—but it usually does.

Extensions: Nope

- One very popular feature of the desktop Chrome browser is its vast library of extensions, such as ad blockers and password managers. Although there is often speculation about if and when Google will implement extensions for the Android version of Chrome, at this time there is no way to run Chrome extensions on your Galaxy.

Clearing History and Cookies

- To clear your private browsing data, tap ⋮ → "Settings" → "Privacy." Tap "Clear browsing data" at the bottom of the screen, select the types of data you want to delete, and then tap "Clear."

Tweaking Other Chrome Settings

Chrome has additional settings and features we haven't discussed in detail. Some of these include:

- Changing the **default search engine** to something other than Google;
- Enabling/disabling **save passwords** and **autofill** (of order forms, etc.) of your personal information;
- Setting a **home page**;
- Enabling web page **pre-fetching** on Wi-Fi (anticipates links you might click and caches their content to speed up browsing);
- Using Google's Data Saver feature to **compress your browsing data** and save bandwidth on your cell plan;
- Blocking **pop-up windows**;
- Disabling **JavaScript**;
- Configuring foreign language **translation settings**;
- and more.

You can investigate and customize these options yourself by tapping ⋮ → "Settings" and exploring the settings sub-menus.

Making Calls

- Calls are made through the Phone app. It's in your app tray and app drawer by default.

Making and Ending Calls

- To place a call, open the Phone app and tap the keypad icon (▦) if the keypad is not displayed on the screen.

- Dial the outgoing number as you would on a normal phone, and then tap 📞 to place the call.

- If you make an error while entering the number, tap ⊗ to delete the last digit entered.

There are several other ways to make calls as well:

- Tap the "Log" tab to view recent calls, tap a name or number, and then 📞.
- Tap the "Favorites" tab to view your starred contacts, tap a contact's name, and then 📞.

- Tap the "Contacts" tab to view your entire phone book, tap a contact's name, and then 📞.

- To speed dial a contact, see the Speed Dial (p. 108) section below.
- Voice dial a contact using Google Now (p. 174) or S Voice (p. 181).
- Tap a 10-digit phone number on a webpage in Internet or Chrome, and then 📞.

> ⭐ **TIP:** *Swipe left on any contact in your call log or Contacts to quickly text message them, or swipe right to call them. If you don't like this feature, disable it in Phone → "More" → "Settings" → "Swipe to call or send messages."*

Answering and Rejecting Calls

- To answer an incoming call, tap and hold 📞 and drag it right.
- To reject an incoming call, tap and hold 📞 and drag it left.

- Alternatively, swipe the "Reject call with message" tab upward, and then tap the message you wish to send. Your Galaxy rejects the call and dispatches a text message to the caller.

- To customize rejection messages, go to Phone → "More" → "Settings" → "Call blocking" → "Call-reject messages."

> ⭐ **TIP:** *If you receive a call while an app is open on your screen, you only see a small pop-up instead of a full-screen notification that kicks you out of your app: In this case, just tap "Answer" or "Reject." No swiping necessary.*

In-Call Controls

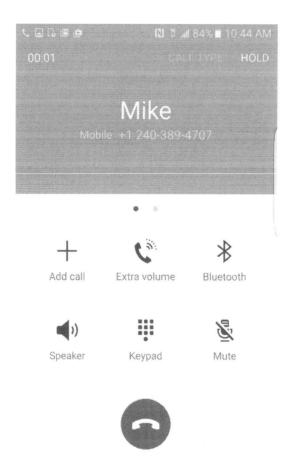

When you're in an active call, you have the following options:

- "Add call" dials in a third party.
- "Extra volume" boosts the call volume above the normal maximum volume.
- "Bluetooth" switches the call to a Bluetooth headset or car stereo, if one has been paired (p. 215).

- "Speaker" switches to speakerphone.
- "Keypad" shows a number pad so you can enter numbers on automated phone lines.
- "Mute" turns off your microphone, so the other party cannot hear you.
- Adjust the call volume using the Volume Up and Down buttons.
- Tap ⬭ to see your home screen and open other apps while keeping your call connected.
- Swipe right to access some common apps while on a call (works best when you're using the speakerphone).

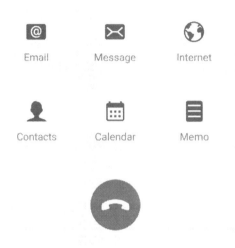

TIP: Notice the "Hold" option in the upper-right-hand corner of the screen. In my experience, Hold doesn't work well on Android. It often causes the call to disconnect. Just use Mute instead—it accomplishes the same thing.

Screening Calls Discreetly

- Sometimes you want to discretely reject a call—let it go to voicemail, but let it ring normally first.
- Obviously all you have to do is not answer—but there's a good trick to know.
- While your Galaxy is ringing, just tap the Volume Down key to silence the ringtone, but let the call continue to voicemail normally. This way, the caller doesn't think you're rejecting their call after one or two rings, and you don't have to listen to the phone ring all the way to voicemail.

Checking and Returning Missed Calls

- When you miss a call, you receive a notification in your notification panel.
- Swipe down the notification panel and tap the notification to view the caller's details and return their call if you wish.
- If you don't see the "Call back" and "Message" shortcuts, place two fingers on the notification and drag down.

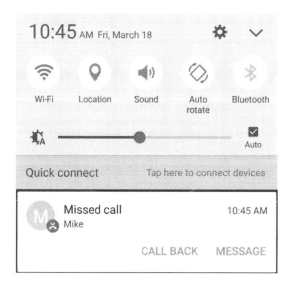

Speed Dial

- To create a new speed dial contact, go to Phone → 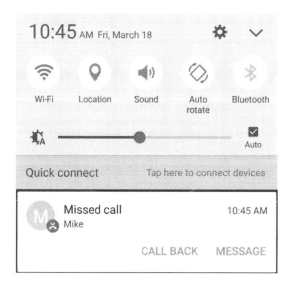 → "More" → "Speed dial." From this page, tap the number to which you wish to assign a contact and select the appropriate contact/phone number from your contacts.
- To dial a speed dial contact after it has been assigned, go to Phone → and dial the speed dial number, holding the last digit until the contact is dialed. For example, to dial the contact associated with speed dial "2," simply tap and hold 2. To dial the contact associated with speed dial "25," tap 2, then tap and hold 5.
- To remove a speed dial contact, go to Phone → → "More" → "Speed dial." From this page, tap ▬ next to the speed dial contact you wish to remove.

Video Calls

- At the time of writing, some carriers are rolling out a new video calling feature that works with recent Samsung phones, such as the S7, S7 Edge, and the Note 5. This feature is built directly into the Phone app and uses your Galaxy's front camera.

- To place a video call, open the Phone app, dial the intended number, and then tap 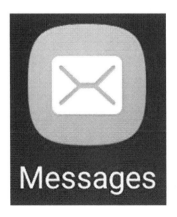 (the camera icon to the right of the call button).
- Although this is a very cool feature, currently you can only video call other Samsung smartphone owners who are on the same carrier as you, so in practice its usefulness may be limited.

> ⭐ *TIP: To video call someone who's not a Samsung user on your carrier, try Google's pre-installed Hangouts app instead. Video calling someone using the Hangouts app only requires that they have an Android device with Hangouts installed.*

Checking Voicemail

- To check your voicemail, go to Phone → ▦. Tap ▣ and follow the prompts. The first time you call your voicemail, you may need to set a PIN and record a greeting depending on your carrier's procedures.

Visual Voicemail

- Depending on your carrier, you may have a visual voicemail app in your app drawer. Visual voicemail apps list your voicemails on-screen like emails and let you selectively listen to or delete them. If your carrier includes such an app, try it out—it's a big step up from traditional voicemail.

Sending Text Messages (SMS) and Picture Messages (MMS)

- Text messages are sent through the Messages app, which is in your app tray by default.

- After you've opened the Messages app, tap an existing conversation thread to open it, or tap 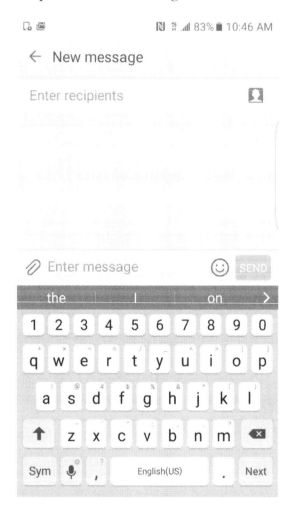 to compose a new text message.

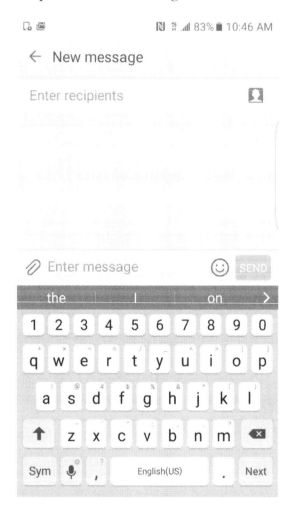

⭐ **TIP:** *To easily change the font size in the Messages app using the volume keys, go to "More" → "Font size." You can also pinch-to-zoom, but only after you've opened a conversation thread—this won't work in the main Messages screen.*

- To specify a recipient, tap in the "Enter recipients" field and type a phone number or name in your contacts.
- Alternatively, tap 🔲 and select a contact from your phone book.
- You can enter multiple recipients. Some carriers support group messaging, meaning that if you include multiple recipients, any replies sent to you are also sent to *all* your original recipients. Be careful with this feature—it's very useful but potentially very awkward if you don't understand it. (To disable this feature, go to "More" →

"Settings" → "More settings" → "Multimedia messages" and turn off "Group conversation.")

- To enter a message, tap in the "Enter message" field and type your message.
- Attach a photo by tapping 📎 → "Gallery" and then selecting a picture and tapping "Done." Alternatively, tap 📎 → "Camera" to take a picture without leaving the Messages app at all. This is how to send a picture message, otherwise known as an MMS.

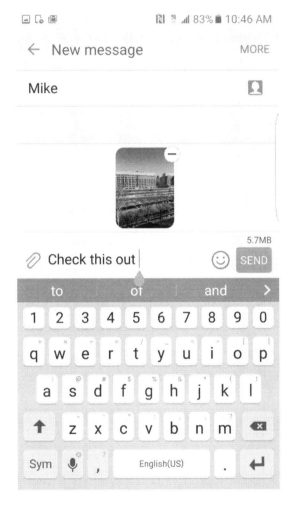

- After you've selected a recipient and composed a message, tap "Send" to dispatch your message.
- When you receive a response to a text message, you receive a notification in your notification panel.

- Tap the notification to open the text message thread in the Messages app, or use the "Call" and "Reply" shortcuts to quickly respond to the text.
- If you don't see the "Call" and "Reply" buttons, place two fingers on the notification and drag down.

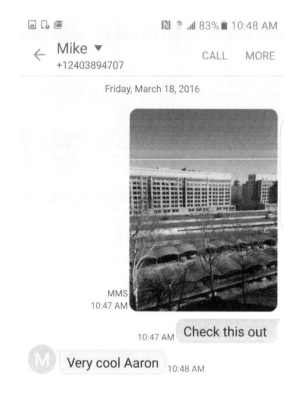

- Compose further replies in the same manner described above.

Setting Up Priority Senders to Text Quickly

- Priority Senders lets you compose new texts to your favorite people with a single tap.
- To set it up, tap "Tap to add priority senders" in the Messages app:

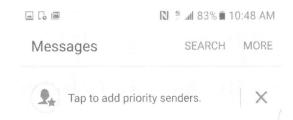

- Locate the contact(s) that you wish to place in your Priority Senders area, select them, and then tap "Done" in the upper-right-hand corner of the screen.
- Your contact(s) appear in the Priority Senders area. Tap one to quickly compose a new text message, or tap ┼ to add additional Priority Senders.

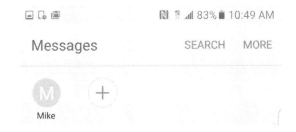

Customizing the Appearance of the Messages App

- To customize the appearance of conversation threads in the Messages app, tap "More" → "Settings" → "Backgrounds." Make your desired changes, and then tap ↰ to save your changes.
- To change the font size inside conversation threads, pinch in and out to zoom. To change the font size on the main Messages screen, tap "More" → "Font size."

Blocking Numbers

- To block a number from sending you texts, open the conversation thread and tap "More" → "Block number."
- To manage your blocked numbers, return to the main Messages screen and tap "More" → "Settings" → "Block messages" → "Block list."

Deleting Messages

- To delete a conversation thread, tap and hold it on the main Messages screen so you see a checkmark next to it. Then tap "Delete."
- To delete a single message inside a conversation thread, tap and hold it and then tap "Delete."

Locking Messages to Prevent Accidental Deletion

- You can lock individual messages inside conversation threads so they cannot accidentally be deleted, even if you attempt to delete the entire thread. (However, entire threads cannot be locked.)
- To do so, tap and hold a single message inside a conversation thread, and then tap "Lock."

Using the Gmail App

- On the S7 and S7 Edge, there are two preloaded apps from which you can send and receive emails: Gmail and Email. Gmail is designed for people who have and regularly use a @gmail.com email address, whereas Email is designed for people who have non-Gmail email addresses.

- However, the Gmail app now supports all email address as well—not just Gmail— and in my opinion it's a better app than Email anyway. So, my advice is to use the Gmail app and completely disregard the Email app regardless of whether you have a @gmail.com email address. The only exception is if you have an Outlook work account you want to set up on your Galaxy. In that case, I suggest using a third-party Outlook client called TouchDown (p. 308).

Setting Up the Gmail Inbox

- When you first launch the Gmail app, you see the following screen.

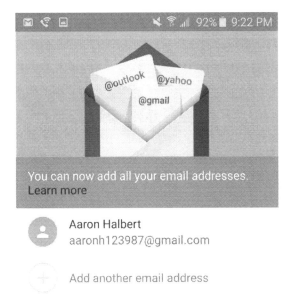

- If you set up your Google account in Chapter 3 (p. 24), your Gmail address is already listed like mine is above.

- To set up additional email addresses for use with the Gmail app, tap "Add another email address."

- To proceed, tap "take me to Gmail."

⭐ **TIP:** *Unlike the Phone and Messages apps, the Gmail app is not in the app tray by default—it's in the app drawer, inside the "Google"* *folder. I suggest creating a shortcut in the app tray or on your home screen so you don't have to open your app drawer every time you want to open your inbox.*

- Welcome to the Gmail inbox. Let's discuss the controls available.

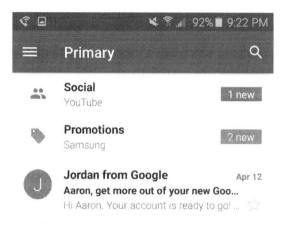

- Tap on any email to open it. Once you open an email, you can <u>reply to it or forward it</u> (p. 119).
- Swipe an email left or right to archive it. If you accidentally archive an email, just tap "Undo." Want to disable this feature? Read <u>here</u> (p. 121).
- To select one or more emails, tap the sender image(s) on the left-hand side of the screen. (If no image is specified, you'll just see the first letter of the sender's name, like the "J" above.) Then, use the controls along the top of the screen to take action on the selected emails.
    - ○ ⬑: Deselect all emails.
    - ○ ⬇: Archive selected emails.

- o ⬜: Delete selected emails.

- o ⬜ / ⬜: Mark email(s) as read or unread, respectively.

- o ⬜: Access additional options, including move, change label, add star, mark important, mute, and report spam.

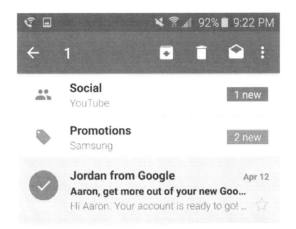

- Swipe from the far left edge of the screen right, or tap ▤ to pull up the main menu. Swipe up and down to scroll through your folders and labels, and tap one to open it. Note that Gmail's settings page is tucked away at the bottom of this menu.

- Tap ⊘ in the lower-right-hand corner of the screen to compose a new email.

- Tap 🔍 to search your emails.

Reading Emails

- When reading an email, the controls at the top of the screen include, from left to right:

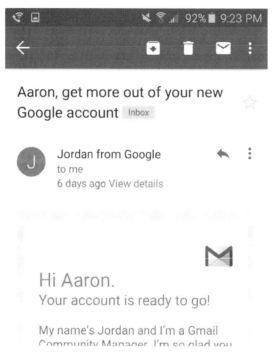

- : Back to inbox.
- : Archive email.
- : Delete email.
- : Mark as unread.
- : Additional options.
- Compose a reply by tapping ↰, or reply-all or forward the email by tapping ⋮ .
- Tap the sender image to create a new contact or add the sender's email address to an existing contact.
- Tap ☆ to star the email.
- Pinch with two fingers to zoom in and out on the email body itself.

Composing and Sending an Email

- When composing a new email, you see a screen like this:

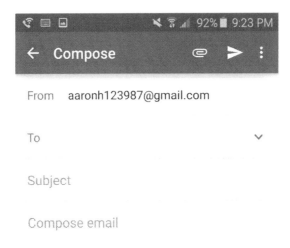

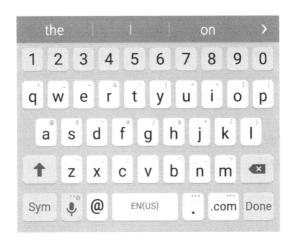

- The "To," "Subject," and "Compose" email fields are self-explanatory.
- After you have composed and addressed your email, attach files to it by tapping
  .

- Tap ⋮ for additional options.
- Send the email with ➤.

- Composing a reply is almost exactly the same process, with one notable difference. Instead of "Compose" in the upper-left-hand corner, you will see "Reply."
- Tap "Reply" to change the mode of the email to reply-all or forward.

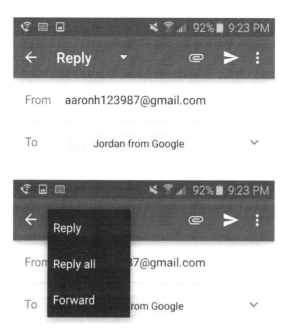

Attaching Files

- On older Android phones, it was only possible to attach image or video files to Gmail messages. Fortunately, this has been corrected and it's now possible to attach nearly any type of file saved on your Galaxy or in your Google Drive.

- To attach a file to a Gmail message, tap ⌫ while composing an email. Choose the appropriate source ("Attach file" lets you select a file saved on your Galaxy's internal memory) and follow the prompts to select the desired file.

Refreshing Your Inbox

- The Gmail app periodically gets clogged up and stops receiving new emails. If this happens, bring it back into sync by refreshing your inbox. In the main inbox view, place your finger in the middle of the screen and drag down. A swirling arrow appears, and when it disappears again, your inbox is in sync. If this does not fix the problem, restart your Galaxy (p. 57).

- A similar problem sometimes occurs when sending a message with a large attachment; it gets stuck in the outbox folder and never sends. If this happens, restart your Galaxy and it will finish sending the email. The Gmail app has been notorious for this behavior for years, and Google has never quite managed to squash the software bug. Fortunately, a restart almost always does the trick.

Storing More Emails Offline

- By default, your Galaxy stores your last 30 days of emails in its internal memory. To access anything older than that, it has to connect to Google's servers. This isn't normally a problem unless you spend a lot of time in dead cell zones. If you do, consider increasing this setting. Tap ▤ → "Settings" → (Your email address) → "Days of mail to sync."

Getting a Notification for Every New Email

- By default, if you receive multiple emails in a short period of time, your Galaxy sounds a notification only the first time. This can be bad if there's an urgent chain of emails, because you might not realize you've received more than one.

- To make your Galaxy sound a notification for every new email, tap ▤ → (Your email address) → "Inbox sound & vibrate" and check "Notify for every message."

Disabling Swipe-to-Archive to Prevent Accidents

- By default, you can swipe an email in your inbox right or left to archive it. While this is convenient, unfortunately it is far too easy to accidentally swipe a message away and miss the window to tap "Undo." Unlike accidentally deleting an email, there is no way to know which email you archived this way! There have been many times where I accidentally archived an email that I knew was important, but couldn't figure out what it was.

- To prevent this, tap ▤ → "Settings" → "General settings" and disable "Swipe actions."

Confirming Before Sending

- In a professional setting, few things are worse than sending an email you didn't mean to send. To avoid this, tap ▤ → "Settings" → "General settings" and enable "Confirm before sending." You'll receive a confirmation dialog every time you attempt to send a message, preventing a potential classic career-ending faux pas. Just make sure not to accidentally reply-all—another classic email mistake.

Customizing Your Inbox Categories

- Google recently introduced a Gmail feature that splits your inbox into various categories such as "Social" and "Promotional."

- If you detest this feature as much as I do, it's easy to switch off. Tap ▤ → "Settings" → (Your email address) → "Inbox categories" and uncheck the categories you don't want.

Setting a Signature

- To set a signature for all emails sent from your Galaxy, tap ▤ → "Settings" → (Your email address) → "Signature."

Muting Conversations

- The Gmail app includes a "mute" feature that automatically archives all future emails in a given conversation, skipping your inbox entirely.
- This is a great feature if you've been CC'd on an ongoing email thread you don't care about.
- To mute a conversation, open it, and tap ⋮ → "Mute."

Managing and Adding Email Accounts

- Want to add a new email address to the Gmail app? Tap ▤ → ▼, then "Add account" or "Manage accounts."
- Remember, the Gmail app now supports all email addresses, not just @gmail.com email addresses.

Tweaking Other Gmail Settings

- Gmail has dozens of settings available that let you customize the interface to work exactly as you please.
- I've already discussed many of the most important settings, but I suggest you explore all Gmail settings to perfectly configure the app for your needs.
- To do so, go to ▤ → "Settings." Some settings are under "General settings" and others are under (your email address), so explore both menus.

Taking Photos with the Camera App

- Photos and videos are taken with the Camera app, found on your home screen.
- The S7 and S7 Edge have a 12-megapixel rear camera with an f/1.7 aperture, 1/2.5" sensor, 4K video, dual-pixel technology, and optical image stabilization (OIS). Their 5-megapixel front camera has a wide-angle lens also with an f/1.7 aperture. Translation: the cameras on the S7 and S7 Edge are *the* best smartphone cameras to date.
- In particular, they excel in low-light scenarios and capture up to 95% more light than the previous generation.

> **TIP:** A discussion of digital photography concepts is outside the scope of this section. If you want to learn more about basic photography concepts like metering and ISO, I suggest Googling.

- By default, the Camera app opens into stills (as opposed to video) mode.

- ![icon]: Expand the quick actions bar. Quick actions include:

  a. ![icon]: Open advanced camera settings.

  b. ![icon]: Set the photo resolution (# of megapixels).

  c. ![icon]: Toggle the flash mode between "always off," "automatic," and "always on."

  d. ![icon]: Set the shutter self-timer.

  e. ![HDR icon]: Enable/disable HDR mode. HDR stands for "High Dynamic Range," and uses software techniques to improve the exposure and color in your photos. Basically, digital cameras capture only a portion of the lighting situations that the human eye can see, and HDR tries to correct this. If your photo includes both very bright and very dark objects, you will normally get either some over-exposed, blown out areas, or some under-exposed, dark areas, or both. HDR helps fix this problem. Experiment with this setting to see what looks best.

  f. ![icon]: Apply filters like film, retro, pastel, etc.

- ![icon]: Indicates the camera is in low-light mode (the device sets this automatically based on the surrounding lighting conditions). Tapping this does nothing.

- ![MODE icon]: Choose from a variety of camera modes, including panorama, selective focus, slow-motion, Video Collage, Live Broadcast, and more. Tap "Download" to get more mode plug-ins from Samsung. There is also a new "Pro" mode that provides on-screen exposure, ISO, and white balance settings. Pro Mode is discussed further below.

- ![icon]: Switch between the front and rear cameras.

- ![icon]: Shutter button. Tap to take a picture, or tap and hold to take burst shots in quick succession.

- ![icon]: Video button. Switches into video mode and starts recording.

- ![icon]: Adjust the beautification filter, which softens facial features. Only available in front camera mode.

- ![icon] (square image in lower-right-hand corner): Open the Gallery app to view previously taken photos.

- ![icon]: Exposure adjustment.

- The circle in the center of the screen is the **autofocus and metering area**. Tap anywhere on the screen to autofocus and meter on it. Tap and hold to autofocus, meter, and lock settings. If you want to lock autofocus only and adjust metering separately, you can do so with Pro Mode.

- To **zoom in or out**, punch with two fingers. Note that zooming is accomplished digitally, not optically, so quality degrades quickly as you zoom in.

Opening the Camera in 0.7 Seconds for Quick Shots

- The S7 and S7 Edge have a fantastic new way to capture fleeting moments.

- Just double-press 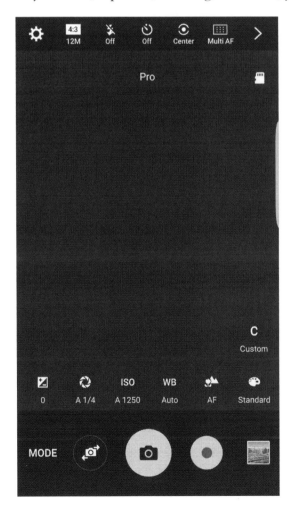 any time, even when the device is off. The Camera app opens in about 0.7 seconds so you don't miss your snapshot.

- I'm a huge fan of this feature. It goes a long way toward solving one of the worst flaws of smartphone cameras—how slow they usually are to launch.

Enabling Advanced Controls with Pro Mode

- Pro Mode is a new feature that provides easy-to-access advanced camera settings. If you like to manually set ISO, exposure, metering, and so on, you'll enjoy Pro Mode.

- To enable Pro Mode, tap "Mode" → 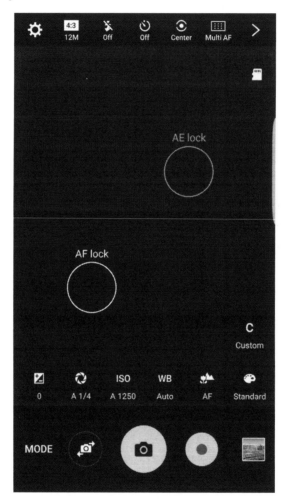.

> ⭐ **TIP:** *Another helpful feature of Pro Mode is autofocus and auto exposure separation. While in Pro Mode, tap and hold to lock the AF and AE. Then release your finger, and tap and hold again to move AE independently of AF.*

Capturing Fast Action Using Burst Shot

- The S7 and S7 Edge are capable of taking multiple shots in rapid succession, which is useful for fast action scenes.
- To use burst shot, tap and hold 📷. A counter appears on the screen, showing how many shots have been taken.

Tagging Your Photos with Location Data

- Ever forget where you took a photo? Try location tagging. It embeds GPS coordinates in your image files.
- To enable it, tap ◤ → ⚙ and turn "Location tags" on.
- You can view these coordinates using an advanced image viewer like Adobe Lightroom on a computer, or by viewing the photo in the <u>Gallery</u> (p. 133) app and tapping "More" → "Details."
- If you enable this feature, remember that GPS information is embedded in the file metadata of any photos you post online! Be careful not to expose personal information by posting photos with your home's GPS coordinates embedded in them.
- Keep in mind that this feature works best when your Location toggle button is switched on in your notification panel and your location method is set to "GPS, Wi-Fi, and mobile networks" in system settings → "Privacy and safety" → "Location" → "Locating method."

Using the Self-Timer for Group Shots

- The self-timer mode is great for taking group shots.
- To use it, tap ◤ → ⏱. Choose your preferred duration. The only tricky part is figuring out how to prop up your Galaxy without a tripod…

Flipping Front Camera Images Automatically

- By default, your Galaxy's front camera takes reverse-mirror-image pictures, meaning that you see selfies the way other people see you—not how you see yourself in a mirror.
- To flip your selfies to mirror-image orientation, tap 📷 to enter front camera mode, then ◤ → ⚙ → "Save pictures as previewed."

Muting the Shutter Sound

- Sometimes you might want to take pictures discreetly. Pretty creepy… but I'm not here to judge.
- To disable the shutter sound, tap ◤ → ⚙ and then turn off "Shutter sound."

Taking Panoramic Shots

- To take a panoramic shot (super-wide-angle), for example of a landscape, tap "Mode" → "Panorama."
- Aim your Galaxy at the far left or right edge of the scene you want to capture.
- Tap ⬜ once, and then slowly move your Galaxy across the scene. Tap ⬜ when you're finished.
- Note that you need to tap "Mode" again to put your camera back into the default "Auto" mode.

Taking HDR Shots

- The S7 and S7 Edge have an HDR mode that simulates the high-saturation, high-dynamic range shots that have recently become popular among digital photographers.
- To use it, tap ◀ → "HDR."
- HDR mode can improve exposure in highlights and shadows, as well as give you punchier, more saturated colors. Keep in mind, though, this HDR mode is all software based, and is therefore more limited than true HDR techniques that involve multiple exposures. It can improve some shots on your but don't expect the same look of HDR photographs taken with DSLRs and processed with dedicated HDR computer software.

Getting Great Bokeh and Editing Bokeh Using Selective Focus

- Selective Focus mode lets you do two different but related things.
- First, it lets you take a photo of an object or person with a blurred background (called "bokeh"), a popular technique in portrait photography.
- Second, it allows you to change the point of focus *after* the photo has been taken, i.e., to blur the foreground and bring the background into focus.
- To take a shot using Selective Focus mode, tap "Mode" → "Selective focus."
- For selective focus mode to work best, the object in the foreground must be within 1.5 feet of the camera, and the background must be at least 4.5 feet beyond the object.
- To change the focal point of a picture after it has been taken, open the photo in the Gallery app and tap 👥 in the center of the screen. You can only do this if you took the picture with Selective Focus mode on.

Applying Color Filters, Including Faded Color, Vintage, and Grayscale

- The camera app has several built-in color filters.
- To use these, tap [⟨] → [☀] and choose the effect you want. You can only use effects while in "Auto" mode.

Setting the Flash Mode

- By default, the flash is always off.
- To change it to always on or automatic, tap [⟨] → [⚡].

Enabling Picture Review

- Want to review each picture after you take it?
- Tap [⟨] → [⚙] and turn on "Review pictures."
- After taking a photo, your Galaxy shows a pop-up window for about 2 seconds. Tap [↩] to dismiss the pop-up window, or [🗑] to delete the image.

Taking Photos Using Voice Control

- Another cool Camera trick is Voice Control.
- Turn it on by tapping [⟨] → [⚙] → "Shooting methods" and turning on "Voice control."
- Once enabled, you can take photos by saying "Smile," "Cheese," "Capture," or "Shoot," or record a video by saying "Record video."
- This is a handy alternative to the self-timer for group shots. It can also help steady your shots, since it eliminates the need to tap the on-screen shutter button.

Taking Photos Using the Volume Buttons

- If you prefer pressing a physical button to take pictures, you're in luck—your Galaxy lets you use either of the volume buttons as your shutter button.
- To enable this feature, tap [⟨] → [⚙] → "Volume keys function." You can also set the volume buttons to zoom or record video.

Taking Selfies with the Heart Rate Sensor

- When you're using the front camera, you can take pictures by quickly tapping your finger on the heart rate sensor, next to the rear camera. It's usually easier to just tap ![camera icon], but try the heart rate sensor method if you find the regular shutter button clumsy.

Tracking a Moving Object with Tracking AF

- If you're taking photos of a moving object, you can automatically track it with Tracking AF. The camera automatically adjusts its focus as the object moves.
- To use Tracking AF, tap ![back icon] → ![settings icon] and turn on "Tracking AF." Then, tap an object to lock onto it. Yellow brackets appear, indicating that tracking is active.

Downloading New Camera Modes

- To download additional camera modes like surround shot (virtual tour), food shot, dual camera, and more, tap "Mode" → "Download."
- You need to be logged into your Samsung account to download these modes. Once installed, these modes are accessed from the "Mode" screen.

Saving Photos in RAW Format

- If you're a digital photography enthusiast, you've no doubt worked with RAW files and post processing software like Adobe Lightroom. Happily, the S7 / S7 Edge support saving RAW files so you can post process your Galaxy's photos just like your DSLR's photos.
- To use this feature, tap "Mode" → "Pro" to enter Pro mode. Then tap ![back icon] → ![settings icon] and enable "Save as RAW file."

Savoring the Moment with Motion Photo

- The S7's new Motion Photo feature saves ~5 seconds of preceding video for each photo you take, so you can go back and see a short video of what happened right before your shot.
- To enable Motion Photo, go to ![back icon] → ![settings icon] → and enable "Motion photo."
- Now, in the Gallery app, any photo taken with Motion Photo enabled have a ![motion photo icon] icon in the upper-right-hand corner. Tap it to watch the video clip.

Capturing Video with the Camera App

- Tap ● to enter video recording mode.

- Recording begins as soon as you enter video mode.
- Tap ▐▐ to pause/resume recording, or ☐ to stop recording and save the video.
- Tap ◉ to take a still shot without interrupting recording.
- Tap ⤺ to exit video mode.

> ⭐ **TIP:** *Counter-intuitively, all video-related settings are adjusted while the Camera app is in stills mode. All video settings are in* ◀ →
> ⚙.

Taking 4K (UHD) Video

- One of the selling points of the S7 / S7 Edge is their ability to capture 4K video for playback on the latest high-resolution TVs. But, there's no obvious 4K setting.
- What you need to do is tap ◀ → ⚙ → "Video size" and change the resolution to UHD 3840x2160 pixels. That's 4K!

Taking Slow-Mo Video

- To take slow-motion video, tap "Mode" while in stills mode and then "Slow motion." The Camera app automatically enters video mode with the chosen effect.

Enabling Video Stabilization

- Video stabilization reduces shake and improves video quality in low-light settings.
- To enable it, tap ◀ → ⚙ and turn on "Video stabilization."

Live Broadcasting to YouTube

- Want to live broadcast camera footage to YouTube to share with friends, family, or followers? The Camera app now has this functionality directly built in.

- To use it, open the Camera app and tap "Mode" → "Live broadcast." The first time you select this option, you have to agree to Samsung's terms of service and grant the Camera app access to your YouTube account. Once this is done, though, you can live broadcast any time just by selecting this setting.

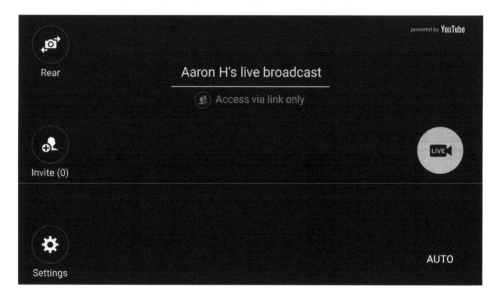

- By default, the stream is private—you have to manually invite users by tapping "Invite" or make your stream public by tapping ⚙. Once you're ready, just tap "LIVE."

Creating a Video Collage

- Video Collages are another new feature on the S7 / S7 Edge.

- A video collage lets you take four six-second videos and combine them into a single six-second video, displayed as a 2x2 grid.

- However, you cannot use previously recorded video, nor can you choose any length of time other than six seconds.

- To create a video collage, tap "Mode" → "Video collage" and tap the record button to begin the process. After each six-second clip, tap the record button again to start the next clip. When you've recorded all four clips, optionally select background music and tap "Save" to complete your video collage.

Viewing Your Photos & Videos with the Gallery App

- So, you've taken some photos or videos using the Camera app and now you want to view them.

- Do so using the Gallery app. You can access it from your app drawer or from the Camera app itself by tapping the thumbnail image in the lower-right-hand corner of the screen.

Navigating the Gallery

- Below is a screenshot of the main Gallery screen.

- Swipe up and down to view your photos and videos. By default, they are sorted by newest to oldest.
- Tap any photo or video thumbnail to open it in full-screen view.
- Tap and hold any photo/video thumbnail to enter Selection Mode (same as tapping "More" → "Edit").
- Tap ⮌ to return to the main screen.
- Tap Time ▼ to sort your photos by time, album, event (location), or category (camera mode), or favorites (only visible when you've starred 1+ photos).
- Tap "Camera" to quickly launch the Camera app.
- Tap "More" to access additional options, including Edit (enters Selection Mode), Share, Search, Animate, Collage, and Help.
- Pinch with two fingers to increase or decrease the size of the photo/video thumbnails.

Selection Mode

- Selection Mode lets you organize and manipulate your photos/videos in batches instead of one at a time.
- To enter Selection Mode, tap and hold a photo/video thumbnail, or tap "More" → "Edit."
- After entering selection mode, select additional photos/videos by tapping their thumbnails.
- Selected photos are indicated by a gray checkmark: ✓ .
- Once one or more photos/videos are selected, tap "Delete" to delete them, "Share" to share them with the Share Via tool (p. 94), or "More" to copy or move them to a different album.
- In the screenshot below, I have selected three thumbnails, indicated by the three checkmarks.

⭐ **TIP:** *To quickly select multiple photos, tap the first thumbnail, hold, and drag your finger up/down/left/right over other thumbnails.*

Viewing and Editing Photos & Videos

- To view a single photo/video and perform basic edits such as rotation and cropping, exit Selection Mode and tap a photo/video once without holding. It opens in full-screen mode:

- Tap anywhere on the photo/video to show/hide the top and bottom menu bars.
- ⬅: Back to main Gallery screen.
- ☆: Star the photo/video and mark it as a favorite. (Filter favorites by tapping Time ▼ in Gallery.)
- **MORE**: View photo/video file details, including location data, start a slideshow, or set it as a contact picture/wallpaper.
- 🪄: Automatically retouch and enhance the photo.
- ⦷: Share photo/video with Share Via (p. 94) tool.

- : Edit photo/video in the Photo/Video Editor (read more below).
- : Delete photo/video.

Advanced Photo/Video Editing with the Photo Editor and Video Editor

- The Photo and Video Editors are adapted from the "Studio" feature on the Galaxy S5 and Note 4. They're much more powerful than the editing tools included with earlier Galaxy devices. For example, they allow you to:
    - o   Rotate, straighten, crop, and resize photos;
    - o   Adjust contrast, saturation, color temperature, hue, and brightness;
    - o   Add tone filters like "vintage" and "grayscale";
    - o   Remove red eye;
    - o   Airbrush faces;
    - o   Add frames;
    - o   Trim video clips;
    - o   Apply filters to video clips;
    - o   Edit audio in video clips;
    - o   … and more.
- The Photo Editor and Video Editor are easy to miss if you don't know they exist.
- To access the Photo Editor, open any photo in the Gallery and tap "Edit."
- To access the Video Editor, open any video in the Gallery app and tap "Edit" → "Video Editor." The first time you attempt to open the Video Editor, you're be prompted to download supporting files from the Galaxy Apps store. Proceed with the download and installation to access the Video Editor.

Creating .GIF Animations

- The Gallery on the S7 / S7 Edge has a new feature that lets you create .GIF animations using photos on your device. Note that its capabilities are limited—there are no text or other special effects.
- To create an animation, go to the main Gallery screen and tap "More" → "Animate." From this screen, select the photos you wish to add to the animation, and then tap "Animate."
- On the next screen, tap, hold, and drag photo thumbnails to reorder them within the animation, and adjust the aspect ratio and animation speed as you see fit.
- When you're finished, tap "Save" to finalize the animation.

Creating Photo Collages

- In addition to creating .GIF animations, you can also create static photo collages, which let you combine up to 5 photos from the Gallery into a single image with a decorative custom layout, border, and background artwork.
- To create a photo collage, go to the main Gallery screen and tap "More" → "Collage." From this screen, select the photos you wish to add to the collage, and then tap "Collage."
- On the next screen, tap, hold, and drag photo thumbnails to reorder them within the collage, and adjust the aspect ratio, layout, border, and background as you see fit.
- Tap "Add" to add additional images, or "Shuffle" to randomize the placement of the photos.
- When you're finished, tap "Save" to finalize the collage.

Managing Contacts

- The Contacts app is your phone book. Use it to store names, numbers, email addresses, and other information for your friends, family, and business contacts.
- The Contacts app is located in your app drawer.
- You can also access your contact list from within the Phone app, but note that the contacts list in the phone app does not have all the same menu settings that are available in the Contacts app.

- From the main Contacts screen, swipe up and down to scroll through your contacts
- Tap a letter along the right edge of the screen to skip to that section.
- Tap a contact to view his or her details.

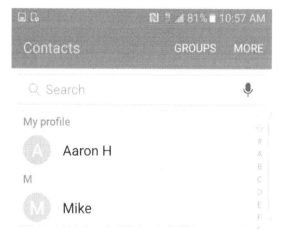

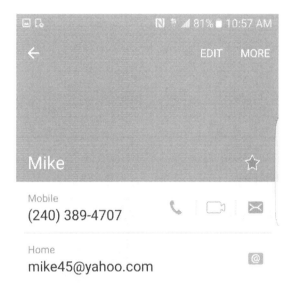

Selection Mode

- Selection Mode lets you organize and manipulate your contacts in batches instead of one at a time.
- To enter Selection Mode, tap and hold a contact.
- After entering Selection Mode, select additional contacts by tapping them. Selected contacts are indicated by an orange checkmark ☑.
- Once one or more contacts are selected, tap "Delete" to delete them, or "Share" to share them with the Share Via tool (p. 94).

Adding New Contacts

- To add a new contact, tap 🗂.
- You are prompted to choose where to save the contact. **I strongly suggest you keep all contacts saved to your Google account** so they are consolidated in one place and can be automatically restored if you ever lose your data or if you upgrade to a new phone.
- I recommend against saving contacts directly to the device or to the SIM card, because if you lose your device, you'll also lose your data.
- I also don't recommend saving contacts to your Samsung account, because they won't be easy to restore if you ever buy a non-Samsung Android device.

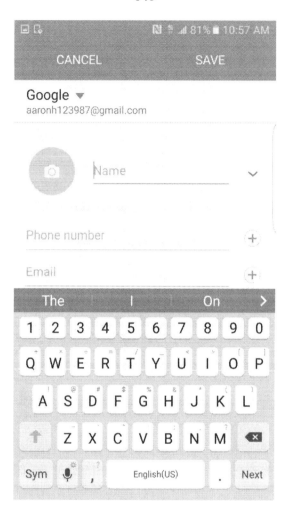

- After selecting a save destination, enter the contact's information.
- Tap ✛ to add additional phone numbers or email addresses to the record.
- Tap 📷 to assign a photo from your Gallery to the contact.
- To add another field like "IM account" or "Organization," scroll to the bottom of the screen and tap "More."
- When you're done, tap "Save."

Editing Existing Contacts

- To edit a contact's details, tap the contact's name and then "Edit."
- Then, follow the instructions in the previous section, "Adding New Contacts."

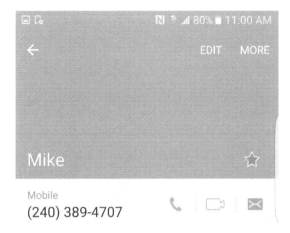

Mobile
(240) 389-4707

Deleting Contacts

- To delete a contact, tap and hold the contact's name on the main Contacts screen to enter Selection Mode, check any other contacts you wish to delete, and then tap "Delete."

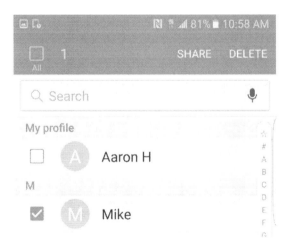

Merging Duplicate Contacts

- When duplicates occur in your contact list, the easiest way to remove them is by going to https://contacts.google.com on your desktop computer and using the Find Duplicates feature. (Of course, this only works if all your contacts are saved to your Google account like I've repeatedly recommended.)

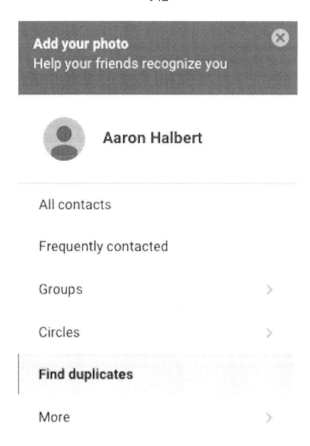

- However, apps like Facebook and LinkedIn can sometimes create duplicate entries in your Galaxy's internal memory. Since these are not saved to Google's servers, Google's contact tools won't detect them.
- Instead, you can use the built-in "Merge contacts" feature, which allows you to manage multiple contacts as a single contact. (However, it does not save the results to your Google account, which is why Google's Find Duplicates feature is a more preferable and permanent solution.)
- To use this feature, tap "More" → "Merge contacts." Select the contacts you want to link and tap "Merge." If you don't see any contacts in the list, it's because no duplicate entries were detected.

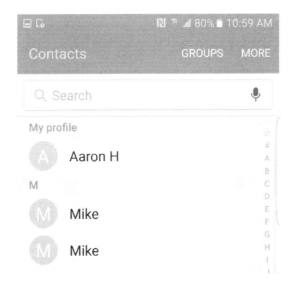

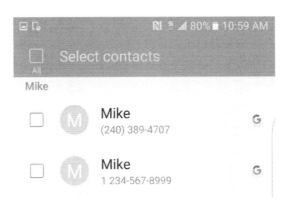

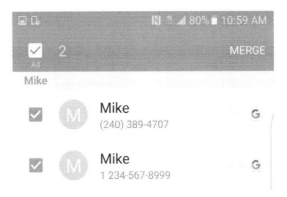

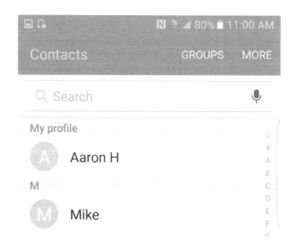

- To unmerge contacts, open a merged contact, tap "View more," and then tap 🔗 . Tap ▬ next to each contact you want to unlink, and then tap ↩ to exit this screen.

Sharing Contacts

- To share a contact, tap a contact in your contact list.
- Then, tap "More" → "Share contact." Select "vCard file (VCF)" to share the contact in the industry standard VCF format, which nearly any modern device can read, including PCs, other Androids, and iPhones.
- Or, select "Text" to send the contact's details as a plain text message without any special formatting.

Setting a Custom Ringtone for a Contact

- To set a unique ringtone for a contact, tap the contact in your contact list.
- Then, tap "Edit" → "More" → "Ringtone." Read more about ringtones here (p. 265).

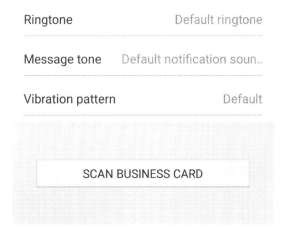

Ringtone	Default ringtone
Message tone	Default notification soun..
Vibration pattern	Default

SCAN BUSINESS CARD

Managing Alarms and Timers

Alarms

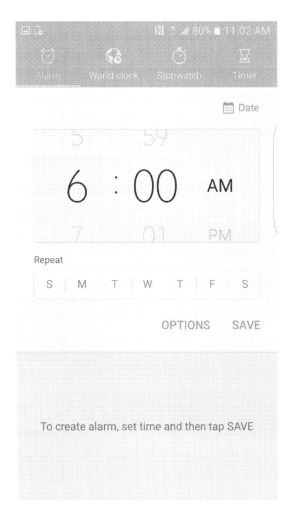

- To set an alarm for a specific time, first tap the "Alarm" tab.

- Use one finger to swipe up and down in the hour, minute, and AM/PM boxes to set the hour and minute for your alarm.

- Tap "Date" to specify a day for the alarm, or tap days in the "Repeat" section to make the alarm recur on certain day(s) of the week.

- Tap "Options" to set the volume, tone, snooze interval, and more.

- If you want to clear everything and start over, tap ⟲ → "Discard."

- To save and activate the alarm, tap "Save."

- Here, I've set an alarm for 7:15am every weekday. I would delete it by tapping ✕, or disable/enable it by tapping ⊙.

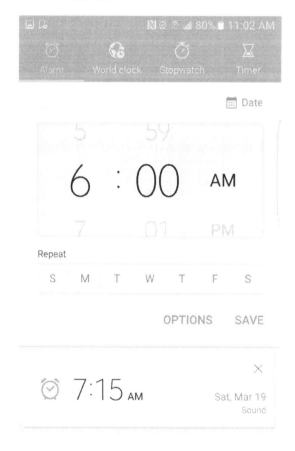

Timers

- To set a timer, tap the "Timer" tab.

- Use one finger to swipe up and down in the hour, minute, and second boxes to set the duration.

- Tap "Start" to start the timer. The alarm goes off when the countdown finishes.

Stopwatch

- To use the stopwatch, tap the "Stopwatch" tab.
- Tap "Start" to begin, "Lap" to record the current time, "Stop" to pause, and "Reset" to zero out the stopwatch.

Playing Music

- There are many ways to play music on your Galaxy.
- You can stream music from apps like Pandora or Spotify, purchase it from Google Play, import your existing MP3 collection to Google Play Music, or just copy your existing MP3 files to your Galaxy.
- Let's talk about each option.

Pandora

- Pandora is a popular music streaming service that lets you stream an unlimited amount of music every month for free.
- However, you don't get to choose every song or artist you listen to. Rather, you create different "stations" based on artists, songs, and genres that you like, and Pandora automatically plays related music it thinks you will like.
- You can only skip 6 songs per station, per hour, up to a total of 24 skips per day.
- On one hand, this can be disappointing if you want to be able to freely pick and choose songs and artists, but on the other hand, it can be an amazing way to discover new music. Either way, because it's completely free, you don't have much to lose.
- The premium version, Pandora One, costs $4.99 per month but eliminates all advertisements, heightens quality, and allows more total skips per day.
- Download Pandora from the Google Play Store.

Spotify

- Spotify is another popular music streaming service that gives you more control than Pandora.
- The free version provides unlimited streaming, and on the mobile app you can listen to any artist's catalog for free on shuffle mode. (That means if you want to only hear one artist, you can—unlike Pandora—but you can't control the exact songs you hear.)
- Like Pandora, you get 6 skips per hour and there are advertisements between songs.

- To remove advertisements and be able to play any song you want, at any time with no skip limit, you must upgrade to Spotify Premium for $9.99 per month. Spotify Premium also has an offline mode, so you can download music to play on the go without using your cellular data.
- Download Spotify from the Google Play Store.

Google Play Music All Access

- All Access is a new service from Google that competes with Spotify. Like Spotify, All Access costs $9.99 per month and has a very competitive catalog.
- It has three main advantages over Spotify: 1) You can also upload your own MP3s, which is very convenient if you have music in your collection that's not available for streaming. Note that you can still upload your MP3s to Google Music for streaming in the Play Music app even if you're not subscribed to All Access—see the "Importing Your Existing Collection" section below for more information. 2) Better Chromecast (p. 315) support. 3) It comes with free YouTube Red, a $9.99/month value that removes YouTube advertisements and grants you access to original YouTube content.
- I subscribed to Spotify for a long time, but I recently switched to Google Play Music All Access, and I've been very happy with it.
- You can sign up for All Access through the Play Music app that comes preloaded on your S7—no additional download required.

Purchasing Music from the Google Play Store

- If you prefer purchasing music instead of streaming it, your best option is the Google Play Store (p. 166). Tracks from the Google Play Store are $1.29 and albums are usually $9.49. For offline listening, you can download purchased tracks to your Galaxy using the Play Music app.
- Although songs bought from Google Play belong to you and have no listening limitations, the cost of a single album is nearly the cost of a full month of All Access, which in my opinion is a *much* better value. Keep this in mind before you buy from Google Play.

Importing Your Existing Collection to Google Music

- If you already have a large library of MP3 or other audio files on your computer, you can upload up to 20,000 songs to Google Music for free. Those songs can then be streamed or downloaded using the Play Music app on your Galaxy.

- To get started with Google Music, go to the link below on your desktop computer and follow the directions to install Google Play Music for Chrome and upload your music collection to the cloud. When you're done, access it using the Google Play Music app on your Galaxy.

> *https://support.google.com/googleplay/answer/4627259?hl=en*
>
> *(Short link: http://goo.gl/mgqV4o)*

Playing MP3 Files

- Finally, if you just want to copy a couple songs or albums from your desktop computer to your Galaxy, you can simply copy the files over USB (p. 272) and play them using Play Music.
- To do so, establish a USB connection with your computer using the directions (p. 272) in Chapter 8. Create a new folder entitled "Music" and copy your MP3 files directly to it.
- On many popular desktop music players like iTunes, you can copy your music files simply by dragging them from the program's interface into the appropriate folder on your device. Note that these files may not play on your Galaxy if they were purchased from a music store that uses digital rights management (DRM).
- After your files are copied, simply open your Play Music app and your music will be ready to play. However, I recommend using the upload tool mentioned above to copy your MP3s to the cloud—much easier than monkeying around with USB transfers.

Customizing Sound Output for Your Ears

- The S7 and S7 Edge have a very interesting and useful feature that performs a mini-hearing test to customize audio output to your ears and headphones.
- To set it up, plug in the pair of headphones you plan to use with the device, go to a quiet room, and start the process by going to system settings → "Sounds and vibration" → "Sound quality and effects" →"Adapt Sound."
- Note that this process tests your ability to hear different frequencies—not volumes—so listen very carefully and tap "Yes" even if you can only barely hear the beeping.
- Once you have completed the hearing test, you can specify whether to use the customized settings for calls, music playback, or both, as well as configure your most frequently used ear if you often use only one ear bud.

- Make sure to try the "Preview Adapt Sound" feature to test the results—it makes a big difference for me, and many other users have reported similarly good results.

Playing Music Through Bluetooth Speakers

- To pair your Galaxy with Bluetooth speakers (e.g., Bluetooth headphones or a car stereo), go to system settings → "Bluetooth."
- If Bluetooth is off, turn it on.
- Put the Bluetooth speakers in pairing/discoverable mode (consult the instruction manual if needed), and wait until the name of the device appears on your Galaxy. Tap it and follow the prompts to pair the devices.
- Your media plays through your Bluetooth speaker as long as Bluetooth is enabled in the notification panel.
- To revert to the internal speaker, just turn the Bluetooth toggle off.

Navigating Using Maps and the GPS

- The Maps app is an excellent co-pilot. It provides directions for driving, walking, bicycling, and public transit, and even offers real-time voice-guided navigation.
- To use it, open the Maps app in your app drawer.

Basic Controls

- Below is a screenshot of the main Maps screen, zoomed out to show the United States.

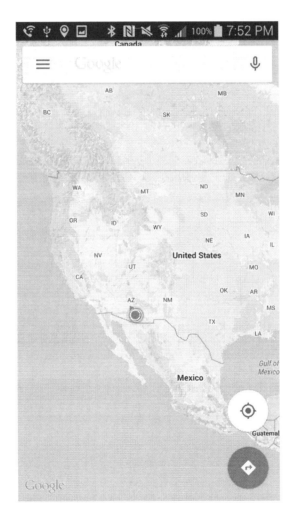

Controls include:

- Pinch to zoom in and out.
- Move your finger around the screen to pan.
- Tap ☰ to open the main menu.

- Tap ⊕ to locate your current position on the map.
- Tap ⟳ to get directions.
- To find locations, addresses, or establishment names, tap the search bar at the top of the screen and type in the name of your destination, or tap ψ and speak your search term. You don't have to enter a specific destination. You can type in a general search term like "Italian restaurants," "gas stations," or "ATMs" and Maps shows you all the results in your area.

The Main Menu

- Access the main Maps menu by tapping ☰ :

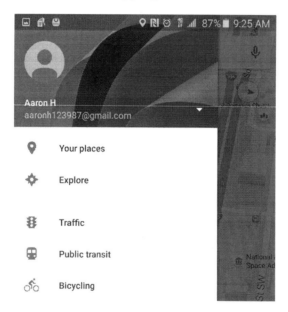

- The options "Traffic" through "Terrain" are all layers. Tap one to enable or disable it. When enabled, information is overlaid on the main map.
- "Your places" allows you to specify your home and work addresses and save maps for offline use (p. 160).
- "Explore" shows you nearby restaurants and attractions.
- "Settings" opens the app's settings page. The most useful settings are discussed later in this section.

Finding Nearby Destinations

- Let's say you're in Tucson, AZ and you want to go to the nearest UPS Store.
- Tap the search bar and enter your search term:

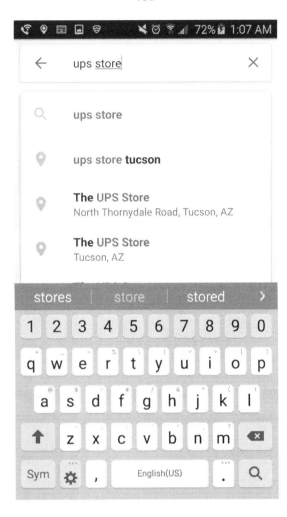

- As you type, results appear below the search bar.
- In this case, the closest UPS Store is on Thornydale Road and is displayed in the list.
- Tap it to view it on a map.

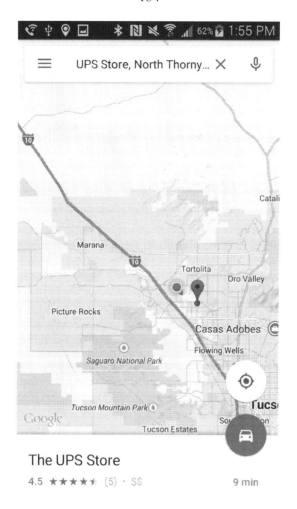

- From this screen, tap to get directions to your destination. If you have previously set a mode of transportation, this icon may be different. Above, it's displayed as a car because I have previously requested driving directions.

- Swipe up the white bottom bar to see detailed location information such as phone number, address, and more. Tap ⤺ to close it and return to the map.

- You can also search for generic keywords instead of specific destination names. For example, here I have searched for nearby pizza joints:

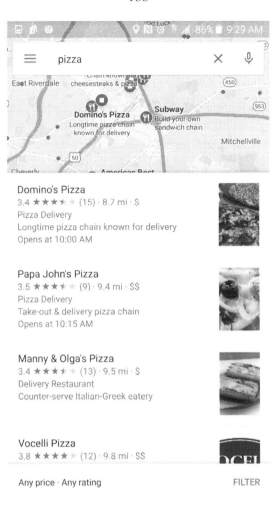

- Tap "Filter" to narrow down your search by hours, price, etc., or tap a location to see detailed location information.

- Tap ✕ to clear the search.

⭐ **TIP:** *If Maps returns search results that aren't near your location, go to the main Maps screen, tap* ⦿ *to refresh your current location, and try your search again.*

Detailed Location Information

- As I just mentioned, detailed location information is accessed tapping a location in "List Results."

- The detailed location information screen looks like this:

- Scroll up and down to see hours, address, the Call button, and so on.

- To get directions to the destination, tap ⟳. Again, this icon may be displayed as a car, bike, etc. depending on how you've previously gotten directions. (In the screenshot above, it's displayed as a car.)

Getting Directions and Using Voice-Guided Turn-by-Turn Navigation

- To get directions to a destination, tap 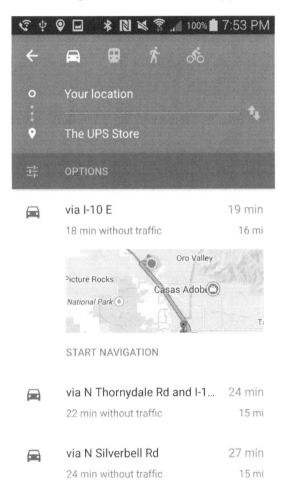 on a <u>detailed location information screen</u> (p. 155) or on the main Maps screen. This screen appears:

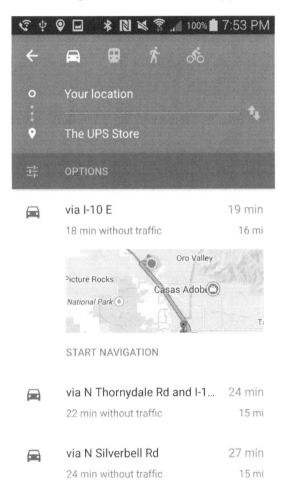

- Tap the icons at the top of the screen to change the mode of transportation, or just below that, edit the starting and ending locations.
- The bottom portion of the screen shows different routes you can specify.
- "Start Navigation" is automatically displayed under the recommended route. Tapping it once immediately starts voice-guided navigation:

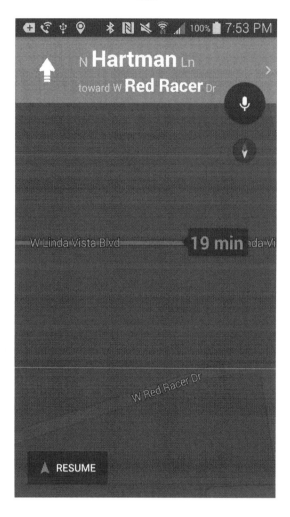

- Alternatively, tap the text for one of the destinations (for example, "via I-10 E") to preview the route without starting voice-guided navigation:

19 min (16 mi)

via I-10 E

- On this preview screen, swipe up the white bottom bar to see text directions without starting navigation.
- Or, to start navigation, tap .

Showing Current Traffic Conditions

- Google collects real-time, live traffic data from DOT sensors installed in roads as well as from other Android users' phones.
- You can easily overlay this information on a map.
- To do so, open the menu by tapping ≡ on the main Maps screen and then tap "Traffic." (Green = clear, yellow = some traffic, red = congested.)
- In most cities this data is surprisingly accurate and up-to-date.

Setting Your Home and Work Locations for Easy Directions

- Set your home and work addresses by tapping ☰ → "Your places"
- Doing so lets you simply type "home" or "work" as starting or ending points when getting directions rather than typing out your entire address. This is also important for Google Now (p. 174) to function optimally.

Improving Your Location Precision

- To find your current location, Maps uses a combination of GPS, cellular, and Wi-Fi data.
- To make sure Maps is taking full advantage of these resources, tap ☰ → "Settings" → "Location accuracy tips." Follow any instructions that it gives you.
- This is particularly useful if you spend a lot of time indoors, because GPS is a line-of-sight technology and is not available in many buildings. Cellular and Wi-Fi location data are needed to correctly identify your location when outside of GPS range.
- As long as you allowed full location access when first configuring your Galaxy in Chapter 3 (p. 24), your location accuracy should already be optimized. If this is the case, you will receive a message notifying you of that, and you will not need to make any changes to your location settings.

Saving Maps for Offline Use

- To save a map for offline use, tap ☰ → "Your places" → "Download a new offline area."
- Pinch to zoom and pan around the map.
- When you have selected the desired area, tap "Download."
- From now on, if you open Maps while you don't have an active data connection, you will still be able to access street-level data for the map region you saved.

Managing Your Schedule with the Calendar App

- Samsung includes a custom Calendar app on the S7 and S7 Edge, which I personally prefer to the Google Calendar (available on the Google Play Store and on "pure" Android devices like the Nexus, but not preloaded on the S7 / S7 Edge). Its tabbed interface is very user-friendly and the layout is intuitive.
- The Calendar is located in your app drawer.

Navigating the Interface

- Upon opening Calendar for the first time, you see the Month view.

Mar 2016 ▾				TODAY	MORE	
Sun	Mon	Tue	Wed	Thu	Fri	Sat
28	29	1	2	3	4	5
6	7	8	9	10	11	12
13	14	15	16	17	(18)	19
20	21	22	23	24	25	26
27	28	29	30	31		

- To switch to a different view, tap ▼ in the upper-left-hand corner of the screen.

Year	2016	TODAY	MORE	
		Thu	Fri	Sat
Month	March	3	4	5
Week	Mar 13 - 19			
Day	Mar 18	10	11	12
Tasks				
13 14 15 16		17	(18)	19

- Personally, I find "Week" view to be the most generally useful, although "Month" and "Day" are helpful for zooming in or out of your schedule.

- "Year" does not display any events, and is mostly only useful for determining the day of the week for a specific date, or tapping a month to jump to it in the "Month" display.

> **TIP:** Like Gmail and Contacts, the Calendar app automatically synchronizes with your Google account. If you log into your Gmail account on your desktop computer and pull up the calendar, you'll see all of the same events in your Calendar app.

Creating a New Event

- To create a new event, tap 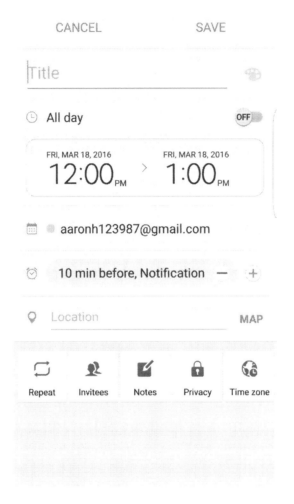.

Options on this screen include:

- **Title:** Name and color-code the event.
- **All Day:** Set the event for a certain day, but do not give it a specific timeframe. Note that you can have other events overlapping with all day events.
- **Start/End:** Specify the starting and ending times/dates for the event.
- **(Your email address):** Tap to change the calendar to which your event should be saved. Useful if you have multiple Google calendars to separate personal and work tasks, etc. If you don't have multiple calendars but want to set them up, go to https://calendar.google.com on your computer. Look for the "My calendars" box on the left-hand side of the screen, click the down arrow, and then "Create new calendar." Any new calendars you create are automatically synced to your Calendar

app. You can view your calendars on your Galaxy by tapping "More" → "Manage calendars," but you can only edit them from your desktop computer.

- **Reminder:** Set one or more reminders for the event. "Notification" pops up a screen on your Galaxy and sounds an alarm, whereas "Email" just sends you an email. I usually set both types of reminders for important appointments.

- **Location:** Enter a location name or tap "Map" to select a location using the Maps app.

- **Repeat:** Set event to repeat every day, week, month, etc. For custom repeat patterns like every other week, or every 20th of the month, tap "Customize."

- **Invitees:** Enter names from your Contacts or email addresses to send email notifications with event details.

- **Notes:** Save miscellaneous text notes related to the event.

- **Privacy:** Specify how the block of time should be displayed on any shared calendars you've joined. For example, you can choose to be shown as "Busy" without revealing any further details about the event.

- **Time Zone:** Specify the time zone for the event. Ensures notifications go off at the correct times even if you're traveling and your Galaxy's clock has been set to a different time zone.

Fill out the necessary information and then tap "Save."

Creating a New Task/To-Do Item

- To add a new task, tap ▼ → "Tasks."
- Tap on the "Enter new task" field and start typing.

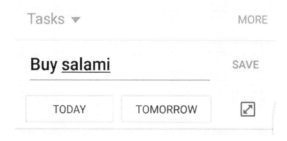

- Tap "Today" or "Tomorrow" to quickly set a due date.
- To set a due date other than today or tomorrow, tap ☑.
- Tap "Save" when you're finished.

- Tasks appear on your calendar along with scheduled events, but unlike events, have a checkbox so you can easily mark them as complete.

Mar 2016 ▾					TODAY	MORE
Sun	Mon	Tue	Wed	Thu	Fri	Sat
		1	2	3	4	5
6	7	8	9	10	11	12
13	14	15	16	17	(18)	19
20	21	22	23	24	25	26
27	28	29	30	31		

Tasks ☐ Buy salami

⭐ *TIP: Unfortunately, there is no way to synchronize tasks in the Calendar app with Google Tasks. If you frequently use the task list in your Gmail account and want to sync it with your Galaxy, I highly recommend the third-party GTasks (p. 301) app.*

Managing and Sharing Events and Tasks

- To manage existing calendar events or tasks, tap them once in Month, Week, or Day mode.

Mar 2016 ▾					TODAY	MORE
Sun	Mon	Tue	Wed	Thu	Fri	Sat
13	14	15	16	(17)	18	19

☐ Buy...

8 AM   Pay h...

9

- To change event or task details, follow the instructions in the previous section, Creating a New Event (p. 163).
- Share the event by tapping "Share." Sharing the event as an ICS file allows the recipient to easily add it to his or her own calendar, whereas sending it as text file simply sends the event information as text in an email.

Searching Events and Tasks

- To search your events and tasks, tap "More" → "Search" and enter your search term.

Installing and Uninstalling Apps with the Google Play Store

- After you've mastered the basics of your Galaxy, you'll want to add new functionality. How? With apps (i.e., programs).
- Personally, I have apps for banking, for Amazon and eBay, for reading news, for managing my passwords, and much more.

> ⭐ **TIP:** Check out Chapter 10 (p. 296) for my list of the 50 all-time best Android apps.

Installing Apps

- The best and only official source for new apps is the Google Play Store.
- You'll find it in your app drawer as the shortcut "Play Store."

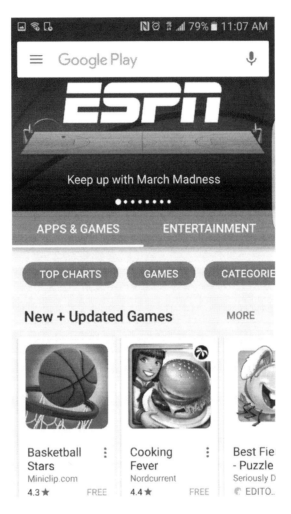

- Tap the "Google Play" field to search for and install new apps.
- If you know the name of the app you want, enter it, or otherwise use keywords (e.g., "shopping list app").
- Alternatively, explore different categories of apps by tapping the green "Categories" button.
- You can also tap "Entertainment" to purchase media (music, movies, etc.) for your Galaxy. Read more about purchasing media here (p. 184).
- Newly installed apps appear in your app drawer.

Updating Apps

- Developers frequently update their apps, and you want to make sure you have the latest versions.
- In the Play Store, tap ☰ → "Settings" and make sure "Auto-update apps" and "App updates available" are turned on.

- With these settings enabled, from time to time you'll see automatic update notifications in your notification panel.

- To manually check for updates at any time, open the Play Store and tap ☰ → "My apps & games." Tap "Update all."

Protecting Yourself from Malware and Viruses

The Google Play Store now has more than 1.5 million apps, and some of these contain malware and viruses that can put your personal data at risk. But you can stay safe as long as you're smart about it. Here's how I recommend protecting yourself.

- First, only install apps found through trusted sources. For example, you can trust apps reviewed on blogs like AndroidCentral.com, as well as those developed by major companies (e.g., Target, Bank of America, etc.). Also, the apps I discuss in Chapter 10 (p. 296) are completely tested and safe. If you're looking for a certain kind of app, run a Google search (e.g., "Android shopping list app") to find apps that are well-reviewed and repeatedly discussed on "best of" lists. Steer clear of apps that you can't find much information about.

- Second, do not download pirated apps. If you're searching Google and you see a paid app being offered for free by a third party, steer clear. Not only is it illegal to download pirated apps, but they also frequently contain malware and viruses, even if the original program is trustworthy.

- Third, pay attention to the number of downloads an app has in the Play Store. In general, apps with hundreds of thousands of downloads or more have been vetted thoroughly enough to be safe. This is not a guarantee, however, and many apps with fewer downloads are also perfectly legitimate.

- Fourth, pay attention to the permissions that an app requires. You'll see this information every time you install an app. Do they make sense given the program's function? For example, if you are downloading a flashlight app that requests full network access, you should be suspicious. I always try to download apps that require minimal permissions, and permissions that make sense for what the app is supposed to do.

- Fifth, you can use antivirus software such as Lookout, which comes preinstalled on the S7 and S7 Edge. Personally, I maintain that if you take reasonable precautions as described above, you don't need antivirus software. I personally disable Lookout on my Galaxy and feel completely secure in doing so, because I follow all the other guidelines explained above.

Branching Out to the Amazon Underground

- Although the Google Play Store is the largest and best source of apps, there's another great place to look for **free** apps in particular—the Amazon Underground, which is built into the Amazon App. Fortunately, the Amazon App happens to be preloaded on the S7 and S7 Edge.

- To download and install free apps from the Amazon Underground, open the Amazon app and tap ≡ → "Underground Apps."

- Tap 🔍 to search for and download free apps in the Amazon Underground.

Installing .APK Files Directly from the Internet

- You can also install .APK app files directly from the Internet, a technique that sometimes comes in handy.

- For example, the F-Droid repository, a third-party app store that contains useful software for <u>rooted</u> (p. 275) devices, is only available as an .APK.

---

https://f-droid.org/

- Installing apps from outside the Google Play Store or Amazon app store is slightly more complicated, but it's easy once you have the hang of it.
- To demonstrate, let's run through an installation of F-Droid.

> **TIP:** *An .APK file is to Android what a .EXE file is to a PC—an executable program (app).*

- In the screenshot below, I open Chrome, visit the URL provided above, and tap the "Download F-Droid" button to download the .APK file.

This type of file can harm your device. ✕
Do you want to keep FDroid.apk
anyway?

CANCEL   OK

- Chrome warns me about downloading apps from outside the Google Play Store. Since I trust the app, I tap "OK."

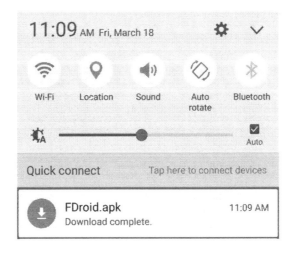

- The download is complete. I tap on the download notification to install the .APK file.
- Next, as shown below, I tap "Settings" to allow my Galaxy to install applications from unknown sources.

Install blocked

For security, your phone is set
to block installation of apps
obtained from unknown sources.

CANCEL   SETTINGS

- I turn on "Unknown sources" to allow installation to continue.

Unknown sources

Allow installation of apps from sources
other than the Play Store.

 OFF

Protect encrypted data

Protect your device by using a screen lock when
your device turns on.

- I tap "OK" on the screen shown below to allow installation to continue.
- Unchecking "Allow this installation only" prevents this warning from appearing again in the future.

Unknown sources

Installing from unknown sources
may be harmful to your device
and personal data. By tapping
OK, you agree that you are solely
responsible for any damage to
your device or loss of data that
may result from using these
applications.

☑ Allow this installation only

CANCEL   OK

- Finally, on the following screen, I tap "Install" to finish installing F-Droid.

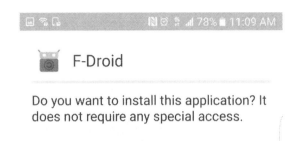

- F-Droid is now available in my app drawer.
- Any other apps installed from an .APK file require a similar process.

Uninstalling Apps

- To uninstall an app, first open the app drawer.
- Tap and hold the app's icon, drag it up to the "Uninstall" area, and release.
- Here, I uninstall F-Droid:

- Tap "Uninstall" on the confirmation dialog box to complete uninstallation.

Getting a Refund and Trying Paid Apps for Free

- The Google Play Store has a two-hour grace period for all purchased apps.
- If you decide you don't want the app within two hours of buying it, go back to its page in the Play Store and tap the "Refund" button.
- This is a great, low-risk way to evaluate paid apps.

Google Now

What Is Google Now?

- Google Now is Google's answer to Apple's Siri—a personal assistant that intelligently interprets your voice commands.
- However, Google Now also includes a proactive approach to information delivery through its card system, something that Siri lacks.
- Using the card system, Google Now delivers notifications to you throughout the day that it thinks will be useful, such as traffic information, flight information, nearby events, and so on.
- Google Now accomplishes this by accessing personal information such as your Gmail inbox, your Google web history, and your location history.
- The more you use Google Now, the more it learns about you and the smarter it gets.

> **TIP:** Launch Google Now by opening the Google app in the Google folder inside your app drawer. In earlier versions of Android, pressing and holding ⬭ launched Google Now. However, in Android 6.0 Marshmallow, pressing and holding ⬭ launches _Now on Tap_ (p. 181) instead.

In total, Google Now has 120+ different cards, some of which include:

- Airbnb
- Car rental
- Coinbase
- Concerts
- Currency
- Developing story & breaking news
- eBay
- ESPNcricinfo
- Event Reminders

- Events
- Fandango
- Flights
- Friends' Birthdays
- Hotels
- Housing
- Lyft
- Mint
- Movies
- Nearby Attractions
- Nearby events
- Nearby photo spots
- New albums
- New movie
- New TV episodes
- News topics
- Next Appointment
- Packages
- Pandora
- Places
- Public alerts
- Public Transit
- Research topic
- Restaurant Reservations
- Shazam
- Sports
- Stocks
- The Economist
- Traffic & Transit
- Translation
- TripAdvisor
- TV
- Walgreens
- Waze
- Weather
- Website updates

- What to watch

- Your Birthday

- Zillow

- … and many more.

- **To summarize, Google Now performs two main functions: (1) proactive information delivery through the card system (information it thinks will be helpful, but that you do not directly request), and (2) reactive information delivery through the voice command system (information that you directly request).**

- If you think about it, this is exactly what you'd want from a personal assistant— things done at your request, or anticipated ahead of time.

Setting up Google Now

- The first time you start Google Now, this intro screen appears:

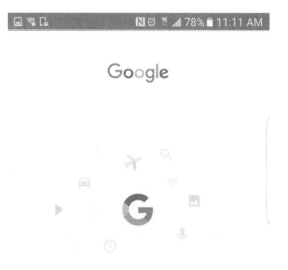

- Tap "Get Started," and then "Yes, I'm in" to enable Google Now.
- From now on, anytime you launch Google Now, you're taken straight to Google Now's main screen:

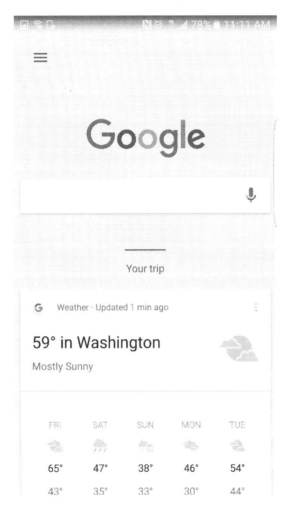

I'll come back to the main Google Now screen in a moment, but first, there are a few settings you need to change to get the most out of Google Now:

- First, make sure all activity controls are turned on so Google Now can effectively learn your information needs. To do this, tap ☰ → "Settings" → "Accounts & privacy" → "Google activity controls" and ensure all the controls are turned on.
- Second, make sure location precision is as high as possible. Go to system settings → "Privacy and safety" → "Location" and make sure "Locating method" is set to GPS, Wi-Fi, and mobile networks.
- Third go to the Maps app and tap ☰ → "Settings" → "Edit home or work" and set your home and work addresses.

- Finally, return to Google Now's main screen and tap ☰ → "Customize." Work through the entire menu, answering questions about your information needs. This helps Google Now get up to speed.
- Now, you're ready to start using Google Now.

Using Google Now's Card/Notification System

- At first, you only have a few general cards such as current weather and nearby places.
- The longer you have Google Now enabled, though, the more it learns about you. It will start to show you more specialized cards and send more relevant notifications to your notification panel.
- In my experience, it takes a few days to a week for Google Now to really kick into gear.
- Even if you don't proactively ask Google Now questions, it still monitors your data in the background and learns about your information needs. For example, if you receive emails with flight reservations or package tracking numbers, Google Now sends you flight information notifications and tracks your packages automatically. It also monitors your calendar and reminds you about upcoming events.
- However, if you *do* ask Google Now a lot of questions, it learns even more about you. For example, if you run a few searches for your favorite sports team's scores, you'll soon receive a new card with your team's scores.
- If you want to stop receiving a certain type of notification—for example, nearby attractions—open Google Now and find the relevant card. Tap the three-dot ⋮ icon next to it and tell Google Now you're not interested.

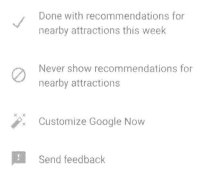

TIP: Dismissing cards by swiping them left or right does not tell Google that you're disinterested. It simply hides them until the next time they're updated.

Using Google Now's Voice Command System

- Now, let's talk about the voice command system, Google Now's other main feature.
- To prepare Google Now for a voice command, open Google Now, and then say "OK, Google" out loud. The following screen appears, indicating you can proceed with your command or inquiry:

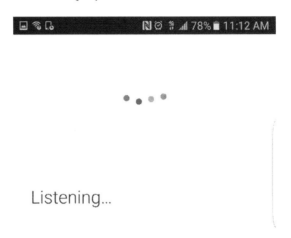

- Below are the results of a couple inquiries I spoke to Google Now, to give you an idea of the types of information it can provide.

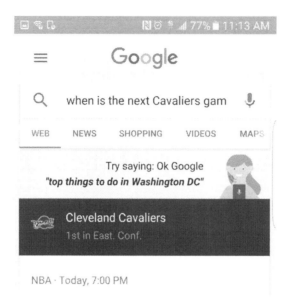

Here is a list of voice commands for you to try. Google is always adding more capabilities, so even if you don't see something on this list, try it.

- "Set an alarm for seven A.M."
- "Wake me up tomorrow at seven."
- "Schedule a meeting at 9 A.M. Thursday morning with John from Microsoft."
- "Will it rain tomorrow?"
- "How many Japanese yen are in three hundred U.S. dollars?"
- "Remind me to buy laundry detergent the next time I'm at Safeway."
- "Send a text message to Craig Johnston saying word up."
- "Driving directions to the nearest Safeway."
- "Call Target."
- "What time is it in London?"
- "Navigate to Yellowstone National Park."
- "Open (app name)."
- "Play (song name)."
- "What am I listening to?" (Google Now will listen through the microphone)
- "Show all hotels near me."

TIP: On the S7 and S7 Edge, you can enable "OK, Google" voice commands on any screen, including in apps. To do so, tap ☰ → "Settings" → "Voice" → "'Ok Google' Detection" and enable "From any screen."

Privacy Concerns

- Using Google Now requires a good deal of trust on your part, because it requires access to so much personal data.

- My position, however, is that you might as well trust Google. I'm not necessarily saying Google is benevolent—just that their interest is in making money, not being Big Brother. If you don't trust Google, you should probably not use a Galaxy smartphone at all.

- Obviously, you have to make your own decision, and enabling Google Now allows Google to track and centralize a lot more information about you. Personally, I've made the decision that the pros outweigh the cons—at least for now.

Disabling Google Now

- If you've had enough of Google Now and want to disable it, tap ≡ → "Settings" → "Accounts & privacy" → "Google Account" → "Sign out."

S Voice: A Weak Competitor

- Samsung packages the S7 and S7 Edge with its own Google Now competitor called S Voice.

- It has many of the voice command features of Google Now, but no card system.

- A year or two ago, I liked S Voice and praised some of its advantages vs. Google Now, especially its voice recognition accuracy.

- However, as of 2016, Google Now has pretty thoroughly slayed S Voice. It doesn't seem like developing S Voice is a priority for Samsung, and it's been de-emphasized on the S7 and S7 Edge compared to earlier Galaxy models.

- I suggest sticking with Google Now, but if you want to try S Voice, you can find it in your app drawer inside the "Samsung" folder.

Now on Tap—New in Android 6.0 Marshmallow

- Last but not least is Now on Tap, a new Android 6.0 Marshmallow Google Now feature.

- Now on Tap is accessed by pressing and holding ⬭.

- It reads the contents of your screen, and tries to provide information it thinks will be helpful.

- For example, if it detects the name of a nearby business, it provides shortcuts to navigate to the business using the Maps app, or to call it. If it detects the name of a currently playing movie, it provides you movie information.

- At the very least, it's a super-fast way to Google anything, as it always shows you a Google button. Now on Tap isn't perfect yet, but it works surprisingly well and will only continue to get better.

Viewing and Editing Microsoft Office Documents

- The S7 and S7 Edge don't come preloaded with an office suite, but if you need one, I recommend downloading the new, official Microsoft Word, Excel, and PowerPoint Android apps from the Google Play Store.

- These apps have been a long time coming from Microsoft, and replace the unofficial Office alternatives that used to be the only game in town, such as Hancom Office and Polaris Office.

- While it's a matter of opinion whether the official Office for Android apps are as nicely designed and easy to use as their unofficial counterparts, one thing is certain: the official Microsoft apps have a monopoly on file compatibility. Anyone who's ever tried editing an Office document in an alternative office program knows that results vary greatly and document formatting is easily corrupted, and this was certainly true of Hancom, Polaris, etc. The official Office apps, however, have near 100% compatibility, even with complex file layouts. This is incredibly helpful for when you just need to make a quick edit on-the-go and email your document to a colleague.

- Let me level with you, though—even though the new Office apps have nearly perfect file compatibility, chances are you're going to be mostly viewing documents, not creating them. No matter how good mobile office suites get, it's just not possible to do serious work on a smartphone screen.

- **Note:** The first time you launch Word, Excel, or PowerPoint, you're prompted to sign up for a Microsoft account. This step is entirely optional, but if you do sign up for one, you're able to easily save your documents to OneDrive, Microsoft's cloud storage service, so your documents are backed up to the cloud. However, Office also integrates with Google Drive, which I think is superior to OneDrive, so I recommend skipping the Microsoft account. Plus, since every Google account comes with Drive, it's one less account to create and keep track of. So, tap "Open" → "Add a place" and link your Google account with Office so your documents are saved to your Google Drive. Read more about the advantages of cloud storage <u>here</u> (p. 250).

Creating or Opening Documents

- To begin, open the desired app (Word, Excel, or PowerPoint) from your app drawer.
- Tap "New" to choose a new document template, or "Open" to edit an existing document. Note that Office integrates with cloud storage apps like Dropbox, Google Drive, and OneDrive, and you can easily open files from these sources after tapping "Open."
- Recently edited documents appear below "Open" and "New" as shown below.

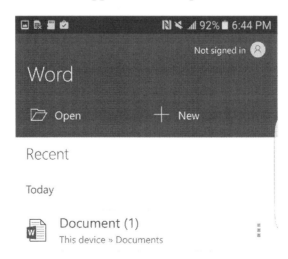

Editing Documents

- This is Office's editing screen. The screenshot below is of Microsoft Word, but the controls are similar for Excel and PowerPoint.

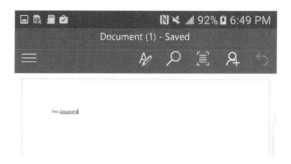

Controls on the editing screen include:

- Tap once anywhere in the document to position the cursor.
- Tap and hold to open a pop-up menu, from which you can choose to cut, copy paste, edit text, etc.
- ▤: Open the menu to save, share, print, etc.
- ✎: Open the text formatting panel.
- ◯: Search for text within file.
- ▤: View document in mobile-reflow style, formatted to fit your Galaxy's screen. Tap again to return to standard view.
- ♙: Share the document using the Share Via tool (p. 94).
- ↺: Undo last change.

Enjoying Movies, Books, Magazines and Other Media on Your Galaxy

> ⭐ **TIP:** *The following section is a little more abstract than previous ones. In this section, I'm not going to give you step-by-step directions for using particular media apps. There are so many that it would be impossible. Instead, I'm going to give you the 10,000-foot view, set you on the right path, and leave the details up to you. If you've mastered everything so far, this will be a piece of cake.*

- The S7 and S7 Edge have tremendous potential as entertainment and media consumption devices. But before you can use them that way, you have to decide where that media is going to come from. (It's not going to magically appear by itself.)

- Broadly, you have two choices: 1) from Google, and 2) not from Google. Which one makes the most sense for you? Let's talk about it.

Google's Media Apps & the Google Play Store

- The S7 and S7 Edge come preloaded with two Google media apps: Play Music and Play Movies & TV. (You can also download Play Books, Play Games, and Play Newsstand from the Play Store.)

- Each of these apps is designed to view media purchased from the Play Store. You see, the Play Store doesn't just contain Android apps, but also books, music, movies, TV shows, and more. Google has huge media catalogs—all of the big-name entertainment you'd expect. It's a simple process: purchase and download media from the Play Store, then view it using the respective Play app. Play Music for music, Play Books for e-books, and so on.

- In my opinion, Google Play is an excellent way to get entertainment media for your Galaxy. The prices are affordable, the selection is huge, and the Play Store conveniently consolidates your entire media collection in one spot.

- Unless you have very unusual and exotic tastes, you'll likely find the books, movies, TV shows, and music you want on Google Play. Want to watch Breaking Bad? Buy episodes in the Play Store and watch them in the Play Movies & TV app. Want to read 1984? Buy it in the Play Store, and read it in the Play Books app. Want to read the New York Times? Buy a subscription in the Play Store and read it with the Play Newsstand app. Want to listen to the Eagles? Buy an Eagles album in the Play Store and listen to it with the Play Music app. (Or better yet, subscribe to Google Play Music All Access (p. 147)—a much better value than *buying* music.)

Mad Men
AMC

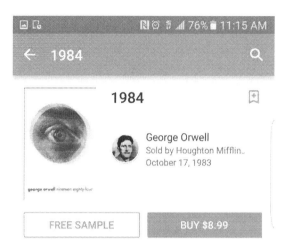

- These apps are all-in-one packages; you don't need to mess with additional apps to enjoy the media you purchase from Google. If you buy into Google's system like they want you to, you'll be rewarded with a nice and easy experience.

- Better yet, you can enjoy all your media using your desktop computer too at https://play.google.com/store, as well as any future Android devices you purchase. You're not just getting one-off copies for your S7 or S7 Edge, you're building a permanent collection.

Non-Google Play Media Solutions

- So if Google's media ecosystem is so accessible and easy to use, why would you ever need anything else?

- Well, let's say you already have a Kindle for reading eBooks, and you have a DVD movie collection. In this case, you might *not* want to build a media collection in Google Play because you're already invested in other platforms and it would not make sense to fragment or duplicate your collections. (If you already have a DVD, why would you want to pay twice to buy a digital copy on Google Play?) In this case, you'd probably want to download the free Amazon Kindle app to access your eBook collection, and maybe use a generic third-party video app like MX Player (p. 302) to view ripped DVD files you've copied to your Galaxy via USB (p. 272).

- Of course, there are Android apps for almost every media provider out there. Have a Netflix subscription? Download the Netflix (p. 303) app from the Google Play Store, free of charge. Have a HBO GO subscription? There's an app for that, too. Want to get a Pandora (p. 147) subscription instead of subscribing to Google Play Music All Access? You're set. Already have a huge library of MP3s? You'll find plenty of great third-party MP3 players on the Google Play Store. Just want to stick to good old free YouTube? Go for it.

Make Your Choice

- The bottom line is that the field is wide open in terms of how you want to obtain media and enjoy it on your Galaxy.

- If you haven't already invested in other platforms, Google Play is a great place to start building a media collection. Google makes it incredibly easy to purchase, organize, and enjoy media on your Galaxy.

- But if you've already invested in other platforms, you can get the apps you need to enjoy your existing media collections on your Galaxy, regardless of where they came from.

- Or, if it makes the most sense for you, you certainly can do a combination of the two. For example, there's nothing wrong with subscribing to Netflix and using Google Play to buy movies you can't find on Netflix.

- You just want to be a little strategic about it, so you don't end up with a media collection that's scattered across a million different platforms.

Chapter 6: The Edge Screen (S7 Edge)

- The S7 Edge sports a sleek, modern design with a screen that curves on the left and right edges. Samsung calls this the Edge Screen, and it brings two things to the table.

- First, aesthetics. Aesthetically, it's new and exciting—it looks different than all the other phones on the market.

- Second, functionality. The Edge Screen adds several features that take advantage of its unique curved screen. Samsung claims these features improve upon the first-generation Edge Screen on the Galaxy S6 Edge.

- In this chapter, I discuss these Edge-specific features.

Apps Edge

- Apps Edge is, in my opinion, the most useful Edge Screen feature. It gives you a way to quickly launch your favorite apps.
- To open Apps Edge, just swipe the Edge panel handle toward the center of the screen. Then, tap any app's icon to launch it.

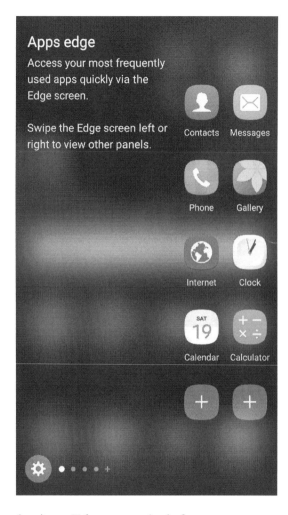

Additional controls on the Apps Edge screen include:

- Tap, drag, and hold apps on the Apps Edge screen to re-order them.

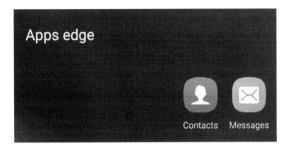

- Tap a "+" to add an app to Apps Edge if you haven't already added the maximum of 10 apps. After tapping "+", tap, drag, and hold apps to add them to empty spaces on the Apps Edge screen. Or, tap "-" to remove apps from the Apps Edge screen.

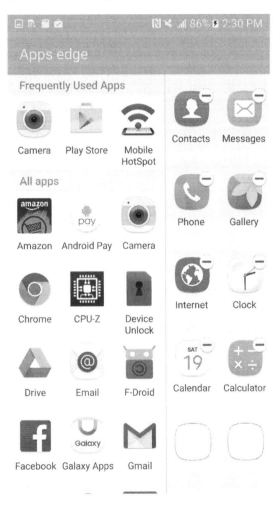

- Swipe right to access Tasks Edge.
- Tap ⚙ to access Edge Screen settings.

Tasks Edge

- Swipe right once from the Apps Edge screen to access Tasks Edge.

- Tasks Edge looks very similar to Apps Edge but works slightly differently. Instead of offering shortcuts to open apps, it offers shortcuts to trigger *specific actions within apps*.

- For example, Tasks Edge has a default "Compose message" shortcut that not only opens the Messages app, but immediately gives you a blank text message to start composing. Another default shortcut is "Take selfie," which opens the Camera app to the front camera.

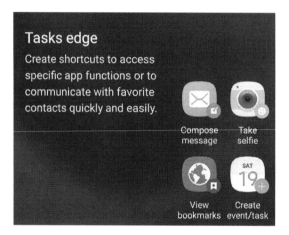

- Unfortunately, Tasks Edge is limited because it only works with select apps (Calendar, Camera, Clock, Contacts, Email, Gallery, Internet, Memo, Messages, and Phone), and only has 2-4 tasks per app for a total of about 25 tasks. If you want to set up a task that's not among these 25—you're out of luck. There's no way to brew your own tasks for Tasks Edge.

Additional controls on the Tasks Edge screen include:

- Tap, drag, and hold tasks on the Tasks Edge screen to re-order them.

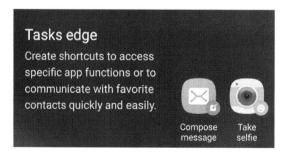

- Tap a "+" to add a task to Tasks Edge if you haven't already added the maximum of 10 tasks. After tapping "+", tap, drag, and hold tasks to add them to empty spaces on the Tasks Edge screen. Or, tap "-" to remove tasks from the Tasks Edge screen.

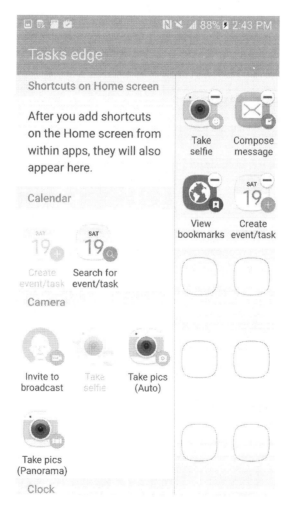

- Swipe left to access Apps Edge, or right to access People Edge.
- Tap ⚙ to access Edge Screen settings.

People Edge

- Swipe right once from the Tasks Edge screen to access People Edge.
- People Edge lets you specify up to 5 of your most important contacts and associate them with custom colors. These colors are used when you receive Edge Lighting notifications and People Edge notifications (more on these soon).

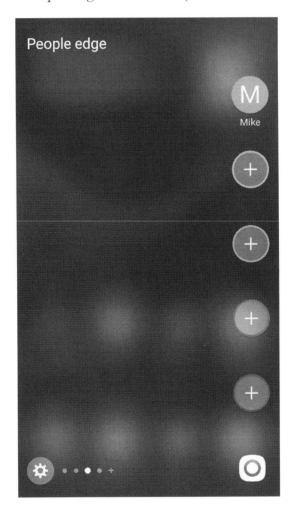

Controls on the People Edge screen include:

- Tap a "+" to add a contact to People Edge if you haven't already added the maximum of 5 contacts.
- Tap a contact and then ☎ or ✉ to call or text message him or her:

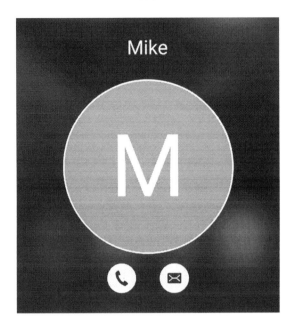

- Tap ○ to start OnCircle, a very gimmicky social media feature based on sending emoticons to your friends, that I suggest you avoid.
- Swipe left to access Tasks Edge, or right to access Yahoo News.
- Tap ☼ to access Edge Screen settings.

People Edge Notifications

- When you have a missed call or text message from a People Edge contact, an additional colored tab appears along the right-hand edge of the screen (the People Edge color you assigned to that contact):

- Swipe it left to view the notification and call, text, or email the contact.

__Edge Lighting__

- With Edge Lighting enabled, the curved edges of the S7 Edge's display light up to get your attention when you receive a call or notification. It's primarily meant to be used with the device face down on a table—thanks to the screen's curves, you can see the light peeking out from the edge of the device.

- In this way, Edge Lighting is a discrete way to monitor your phone while it's sitting on the table at dinner, at meetings, etc. Edge Lighting even works when the S7 Edge is completely muted, so it'll illuminate without intrusively beeping or vibrating.

- To enable Edge Lighting, go to system settings → "Edge screen" → "Edge lighting" and turn the slider on.

- You can also enable "Quick reply" here, which lets you reject incoming calls and send a predefined text message to the caller by tapping and holding the heart rate sensor for two seconds while the device is face-down.

- If you've set up People Edge, the color of Edge Lighting matches the contact's designated color.

Edge Feeds

- Edge Feeds, which were called "Information Streams" on the Galaxy S6 Edge, let you view high-priority information on the edge of your screen while the S7 Edge is asleep.

- To activate Edge Feeds while the screen is off, quickly swipe your finger **left-right-left** or **right-left-right** parallel along the edge (i.e., swipe one direction and then quickly back the other way).

- Then, swipe **up and down** perpendicular to the edge to switch between the different streams.

- To enable Edge Feeds, go to system settings → "Edge screen" → "Edge feeds" and turn the slider on.
- Tap ☑ and ☐ to enable or disable feeds, or 🖊 to customize a feed.
- Tap "Download" to get additional feeds from the Samsung app store, or "Reorder" to change the order of the feeds.
- "Edge feed timeout" controls how long a feed is displayed on your screen before it turns off again.

Night Clock

- Night Clock lets the S7 Edge display the time and date along the edge screen while the device is asleep.

- To enable Night Clock, go to system settings → "Display" → "Night clock" and turn the slider on. Set the start and end times.

Customizing the Edge Screen & Downloading More Panels

- To customize the Edge Screen, including which panels are enabled and the position and appearance of the Edge panel handle, go to system settings → "Edge screen" → "Edge panels."

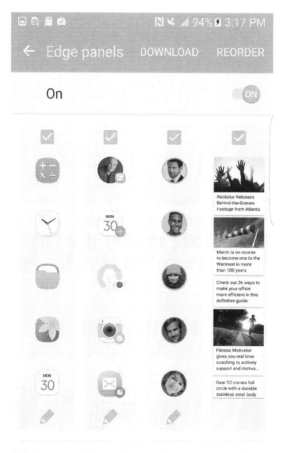

Edge panel handle settings
Right side, Medium, 30% transparency

From this screen you can:

- Enable/disable/reorder panels by tapping ✅, ☐, or "Reorder"
- Edit panels' settings by tapping ✏️
- Change the position/appearance of the Edge panel handle by tapping "Edge panel handle settings"
- Download additional Edge panels from Samsung by tapping "Download"

Chapter 7: Intermediate Tips & Tricks

Congratulations! By now, you should be getting very comfortable with your Galaxy. You've learned how to perform all its basic functions, and now it's time to discuss some intermediate-level tips and tricks.

Multitasking with Multi Window

- Multi Window lets you open two apps at the same time. It's not compatible with all apps, but is compatible with most of the apps preloaded on the S7 / S7 Edge.
- It works two ways: Split Screen View and Pop-Up View.

Split Screen View

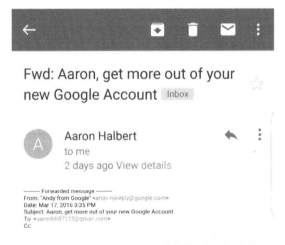

- To launch Split Screen View, tap and hold 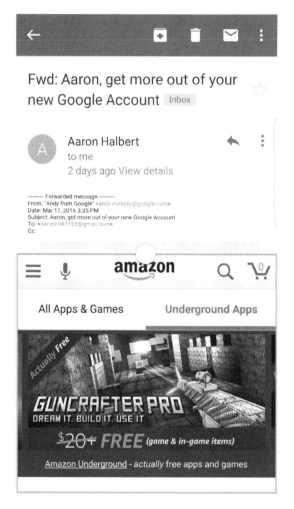.

- Above, I've launched Split Screen View while in the Gmail app. As you can see, the bottom half of the screen is prompting me to open a second app.

- Below, I've tapped Amazon to open it as the second app.

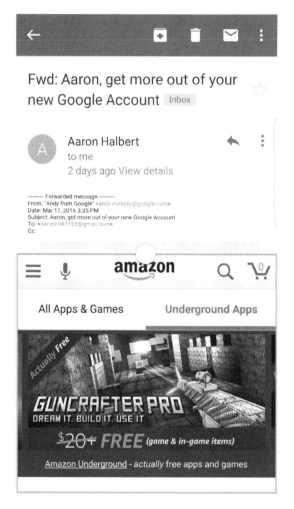

From here, tap the white circle in the center of the screen to access more options:

- Tap the upper or lower app to select it. A blue border indicates which app is selected.

- Tap, hold, and drag the white circle to resize the upper and lower apps.

- : Swap the upper and lower apps.

- : Activate Drag & Drop mode, which lets you drag text or an image from one app to the other.

- : Minimize the selected app into a button.

- : Make the selected app full screen and close the non-selected app.

- ✕: Close the selected app and make the non-selected app full screen.

Buttons and Pop-Up View

- Tapping ⬚ turns the selected app into a button. Here, I've turned the Gmail app into a button:

- Buttons persist on all screens, including the home screen:

- Tap, hold, and drag buttons to relocate them.

- Single-tap a button to open it in Pop-Up View:

From here, tap the white circle at the top of the pop-up to access more options:

- Tap, hold, and drag the white circle to move the pop-up.
-  : Activate Drag & Drop mode, which lets you drag text or an image from one app to another.
-  : Minimize the pop-up into a button again.
-  : Make the pop-up full screen.
- ✕ or ↩ : Close the pop-up.
- ⬭ : Return to the home screen and minimize all pop-ups into buttons.

You can have multiple buttons and/or pop-ups active at once:

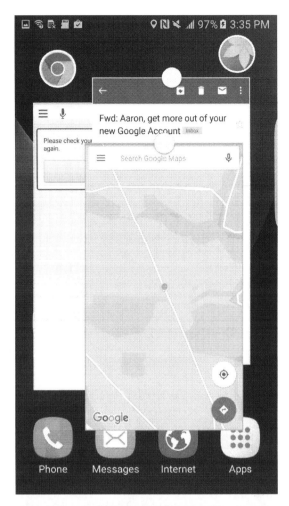

 TIP: *There are a few other useful Multi Window tricks to know. First, you can also open apps in Split Screen View by tapping* → . *Second, you can swipe diagonally from the very top right or top left corner of the screen down to the center of the screen to convert an open app into a pop-up. Third, you can quickly open a recent app*

in Pop-Up View by tapping ⬚ *and then tapping and holding a recent app.*

- If you find yourself accidentally activating Pop-Up View too often, disable it in system settings → "Advanced features" → "Pop-up view gesture."

Securing Your Data

Enabling and Customizing a Lock Screen

- A lock screen keeps your Galaxy safe from unauthorized access. When enabled, your Galaxy locks itself after a specified duration when it's asleep. Next time it's woken, it requires authentication before the lock screen can be cleared and the device can be used. A lock screen prevents anyone from accessing your data if you lose your device.

- To set up a lock screen, go to system settings → "Lock screen and security." Available locking methods include:
    - **Swipe:** This is a zero-security option that only prevents accidental operation in your pocket. On some older Samsung Galaxy phones, you could add widgets to the swipe lock screen, but this feature is absent on the S7 / S7 Edge. In general I suggest you avoid the swipe setting. You probably have a great deal of sensitive information on your device, and if you don't have security measures in place, you will open yourself up to identity theft and other crimes should you lose it. Using a lock screen with a fingerprint, PIN, password, or other feature is worth the minor inconvenience of having to enter it when you power on your Galaxy.
    - **Pattern:** This option lets you unlock your Galaxy by drawing a pattern on a 3x3 grid (with a PIN backup). I suggest a PIN or password instead. It's fairly easy to defeat pattern security by tracing smudges on the screen.
    - **PIN:** This unlock option secures your lock screen with a minimum 4-digit numerical PIN code. There is no maximum PIN length. A PIN is much faster and easier to type than a password on a keyboard, especially when using one hand. Before I started using fingerprint recognition, I used a six-digit PIN code on my Android devices.
    - **Password:** A password works almost exactly like a PIN, but can include letters and special characters in addition to numbers. A password can be more secure than a PIN code but slower and more difficult to type each time you wake your Galaxy.
    - **Fingerprint:** Your Galaxy's home button doubles as a fingerprint reader, and this option allows you to unlock your device by tapping and holding

your finger on it. Personally, this is the option I use. I formerly preferred PIN security but fingerprint recognition is faster, accurate, and very secure.

o **None:** The final option in this menu is to use no lock screen whatsoever. Although this setting is convenient, I suggest carefully thinking through the consequences of losing your phone before using it.

- In addition to choosing a locking method, I suggest putting a "Reward If Found" message in the "Owner Information" field (available in system settings → "Lock screen and security" → "Info and app shortcuts" → "Owner information"), with a phone number to call. This information is prominently displayed on your lock screen.

- Also, make sure to set the locking delay and choose whether to lock instantly with the power key in system settings → "Lock screen and security" → "Secure lock settings" (only visible if you've set a locking method). Personally, I like a 5 second delay with power key locking disabled. That way, if you accidentally hit the power button, you can turn your Galaxy on again without having to re-authenticate yourself.

- On some older Samsung phones, it was possible to add widgets to the lock screen. Unfortunately, this feature isn't available on the S7 / S7 Edge.

- By default, the lock screen shows two app shortcuts, Phone in the lower-left-hand corner and Camera in the lower-right-hand corner. You open these by placing your finger on them and swiping up. You can customize or disable these shortcuts. To do so, go to system settings → "Lock screen and security" → "Info and app shortcuts" → "App shortcuts."

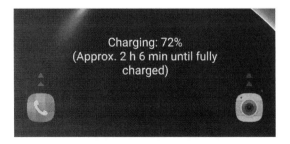

Making Unlocking Easy with Smart Lock

- Android has a new feature called Smart Lock that automatically unlocks your Galaxy under approved conditions. For example, you can set your device to stay unlocked while you're at a certain address or connected to a certain Wi-Fi network or

Bluetooth device. I have my Galaxy set to stay unlocked as long as it's at my house, connected to my car's Bluetooth stereo, or connected to my Pebble watch.

- To set up Smart Lock, go to system settings → "Lock screen and security" → "Secure lock settings" → "Smart Lock." Add trusted devices or trusted places and save your settings. You can also set up trusted voices or on-body detection, but in my opinion these features are much more gimmicky than trusted devices and trusted places.

Internal Storage is Already Encrypted—But Not Your Micro SD!

- The internal storage on your S7 and S7 Edge is encrypted by default—unlike in previous versions of Android, there's no need to take any additional action yourself. All you need to do is enable a lock screen and your data is fully protected. Even if a hacker (or the FBI!) were to extract the memory chip from your phone, they wouldn't be able to read any data on it.

- However, note that your Micro SD card is *not* encrypted by default—and since Micro SD cards are frequently used for storing personal data like photos and videos, I recommend encrypting yours. To do so, go to system settings → "Lock screen and security" → "Encrypt SD card."

Locating, Locking, and Remotely Wiping Your Galaxy

- Google offers a convenient and free remote locate/wipe service called "Android Device Manager."

- To use it effectively, you need to ensure your locating method is set to "GPS, Wi-Fi, and mobile networks" in system settings → "Privacy and safety" → "Location."

TIP: *This feature works well and is totally free. However, I personally use a third-party security app called* Cerberus *(p. 298) that has even more options. Cerberus requires a one-time fee of a few dollars, but in my opinion it's well worth it.*

- To locate your Galaxy, login to your Gmail account on your desktop computer and go to the link below. Click the gear icon in the upper-right-hand corner of the screen, and click "Android Device Manager."

https://play.google.com/store

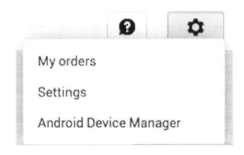

- Google automatically locates your Galaxy and reports its location on a map within a few seconds.

- Google can locate your phone very precisely using a combination of GPS, cellular, and Wi-Fi signals (within 9 meters in the above case).
- Tap "Ring" to have your Galaxy ring at full volume for 5 minutes to help you find it, "Lock" to enable the lock screen with a new password, and "Erase" to wipe all data.

TIP: If you see "Setup Lock & Erase" instead of "Lock" and "Erase," click it and follow the instructions to enable Android Device Manager for your Galaxy. It is VERY important to make sure this feature is set up ahead of time, because there's no way to enable it after your device is lost or stolen. If you lose your phone and you haven't set up this feature ahead of time, you're out of luck.

Hiding Files with Private Mode

- Private Mode hides files that you don't want anyone to accidentally see. It works in only two apps: Gallery and My Files.
- To use it, swipe down the notification panel with two fingers and enable "Private mode."

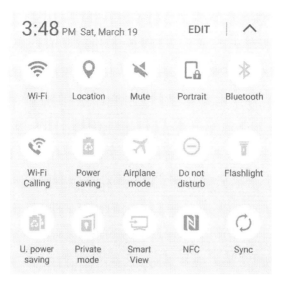

- The first time you enable Private Mode, tap through the tutorial screens and configure an unlock method (it can be different than the method you use to unlock your Galaxy). I suggest fingerprint mode for a good balance of convenience and security.

- Now, in the apps mentioned above, any time you're viewing media and you tap a "More" menu, you will see the option "Move to Private." When you move a file to private storage, it is shown as long as Private Mode is enabled, but completely disappears when Private Mode is disabled, like it never existed.

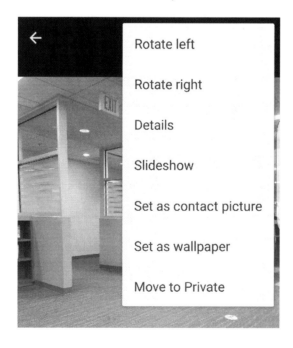

- To view all the files in Private storage, open the app "My Files," swipe down, and tap "Private."

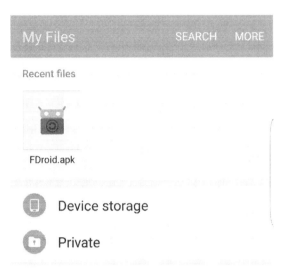

- Remember—you have to turn off the Private Mode toggle button when you're done viewing your private content. If you forget to turn it off, your private files are displayed along with all the others.

⭐ **TIP:** *Enable "Auto off" in Private Mode settings to disable Private Mode any time the screen turns off. That way, if you forget to disable Private Mode, your Galaxy takes care of it for you.*

Pinning Screens to Protect Your Privacy

- Android has a new feature that lets you lock ("pin") an app to the screen, so that nothing outside of that app can be accessed. Use this feature if you need to hand off your phone to someone who you don't want snooping around your personal information.
- To pin a screen, first make sure Pinning is enabled in system settings → "Lock screen and security" → "Other security settings" → "Pin windows."
- Then, to pin an app, open it, tap ⬚ → 📌.

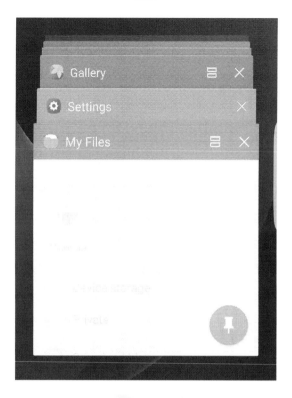

- To unpin a screen, tap and hold and at the same time.

Android Beam, Wi-Fi Direct, NFC, WTF?!?

- The S7 / S7 Edge include several wireless features, and it can be very hard to understand the differences. Each of these features is slightly different, so what exactly does each one do?

NFC & Android Beam

- Let's start with NFC. NFC stands for "Near-Field Communications" and is a fairly new feature in Android smartphones. NFC is basically synonymous with RFID, which you've probably heard of before. RFID tags are tiny chips that store small amounts of data. They're frequently used for passports, inventory tracking in stores, subway passes, and tap-to-pay debit and credit cards. So how does your Galaxy use its NFC chip?
- The first way is through the protocol called "Android Beam," found under the "NFC and payment" menu in system settings. It's used for sending links, images, contacts, and other content to and from other Android devices that have Android Beam. Data transfer is not actually accomplished through NFC, though—rather, the NFC chips

'handshake' with each other, establishing a Bluetooth connection between the two Android Beam-enabled devices.

- In general, you can expect Android Beam to work with stock apps such as the Gallery, Internet, Contacts, and Music. To use it, enable Android Beam in system settings → "NFC and payment" → "Android Beam." Ensure it's also enabled on the receiving device. Then, open the song/contact/photo/etc. you wish to share in its respective app, and place your Galaxy back-to-back with the receiving device. When prompted, tap the content you wish to share and then pull the devices apart to initiate data transfer.

- The second way in which the S7 / S7 Edge use their NFC chip is for tap-to-pay payments through Samsung Pay (p. 230) and other tap-to-pay services.
- Third, the S7 / S7 Edge also use NFC technology to read and write NFC tags, which automate software actions in conjunction with the Samsung TecTiles app (p. 283).

Wi-Fi Direct

- Now let's talk about Wi-Fi Direct, another wireless protocol you may see in your Galaxy's menus. Wi-Fi Direct establishes a direct device-to-device Wi-Fi connection between two Android devices to transfer large files quickly. It uses Wi-Fi instead of Bluetooth for *much* higher data transfer speeds than Android Beam, but has a slightly more complicated setup process.

- To use this feature, use any app's <u>Share Via</u> (p. 94) tool on the sending device and select Wi-Fi Direct. On the receiving device, go to Wi-Fi settings and start Wi-Fi Direct mode.

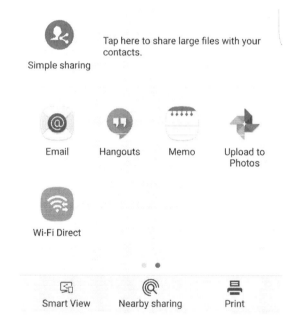

- After tapping Wi-Fi Direct on the Share Via screen, you're prompted to connect to the receiving device, and when successful, the file is automatically transferred. Note that older Android devices may not support Wi-Fi Direct, and even if they do, transfers may not be successful. Wi-Fi Direct is finicky.

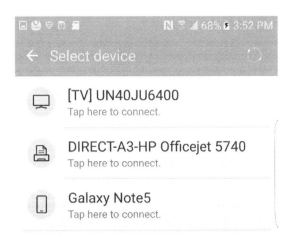

- If you have trouble with Wi-Fi Direct, I suggest checking out SuperBeam (p. 308) (free on the Google Play Store) as a Wi-Fi Direct alternative. SuperBeam is a third-party Wi-Fi beaming app that can send any file to any other Android device that's running SuperBeam, and it doesn't require the receiving device to have Wi-Fi Direct support. It works very reliably and I highly recommend it if you can't get Wi-Fi Direct to work through the Share Via screen.

Pairing with a Bluetooth Device Such as a Headset or Car Stereo

- Whereas Wi-Fi is used to wirelessly connect to the Internet, Bluetooth is used for connecting to accessories such as car stereos, headsets, keyboards & mice, and other mobile devices. Connecting to a Bluetooth device is called "pairing." To pair a device with your Galaxy, make sure Bluetooth is turned on in the notification panel, and then go to system settings → "Bluetooth."

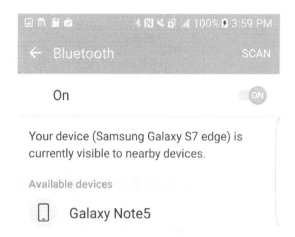

- You'll see devices available for pairing under "Available devices." If you don't see the device you want to connect to, it's most likely because the other device has not been made discoverable. Consult the device's instruction manual for instructions on doing so (may be called "pairing mode" or something similar).
- Tap "Scan" if necessary to re-scan for devices. Once you see the device you want to connect to, tap it and follow the prompts to pair the devices. Confirm the PIN pairing code on both devices to establish a connection.
- Once paired with Bluetooth speakers, your Galaxy automatically plays through them when you're in range and Bluetooth is on. To switch back to the internal speakers, swipe down the notification panel and turn Bluetooth off. For headsets, switch to them while in-call by tapping the "Bluetooth" button, or by using controls on the headset itself.

Setting Up a Wi-Fi Hotspot and Tethering Your Computer

- Your Galaxy's tethering/hotspot feature allows you to share your cellular Internet connection with another device such as a laptop, a desktop, or even another Android device. It makes your Galaxy act as a Wi-Fi router.
- Note that your hotspot feature may not work if it's not included in your service plan. All major U.S. carriers bill wireless hotspots as an add-on that generally runs between $20-30 per month.
- To turn on the hotspot, go to system settings → "Mobile HotSpot and Tethering." Depending on your carrier, this option may have a slightly different name but is still found in system settings.
- After enabling the mobile hotspot, you are prompted to enter a name (SSID) for your network, select a security protocol (choose WPA2 PSK), and specify a

password. You may also see settings that let you hide the SSID, adjust the transmit power, and so on. Do not change these from their defaults unless you have a specific reason to do so.

- After you've created a Wi-Fi network using your wireless hotspot feature, connect to it from your laptop or other device just as you would connect to your home network. If you have trouble connecting, reset your Galaxy by holding the power button and tapping "Restart," and restart the other device as well before trying again.

USB Tethering

- It's also possible to tether your Galaxy's connection via USB instead of Wi-Fi, if you wish.

- In general, this is less convenient than using Wi-Fi tethering and is only advantageous in very select cases. Nevertheless, you have the option.

- To tether via USB, connect your Galaxy to your computer using the included USB cable.

- Go to system settings → "Mobile HotSpot and Tethering" (or similar—exact name may depend on carrier) and enable "USB tethering." On Windows 7, Windows 8, Windows 10, and Linux, your computer automatically connects to the Internet when you plug in your Galaxy via USB. If you have Windows XP or another OS, you may need to take extra steps to get USB tethering working.

- USB tethering does not work at all on Mac OSX, although there is a third-party driver called HoRNDIS to work around this limitation. http://joshuawise.com/horndis

Get further information about USB tethering here:

---

http://android.com/tether

Preventing Extra Charges by Capping Your Data Usage

- If you have a limited amount of data on your cell plan, you can set a hard limit to ensure your Galaxy doesn't rack up overage charges. To set it, go to system settings → "Data usage" and turn on "Set mobile data limit."

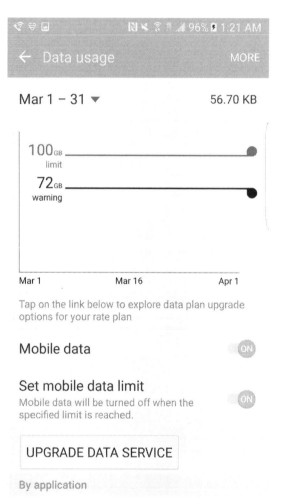

- Set the data usage cycle to match your billing cycle, and then adjust the red slider up and down to specify the maximum amount of cellular data your Galaxy is allowed to use during that period. Adjust the black slider to set a warning level.
- Upon reaching the warning level, you receive a notification in the notification panel, and upon reaching the hard limit, your Galaxy shuts off cellular data completely. Of course, you can always return to this screen and uncheck "Set mobile data limit" if you need to.

Mirroring Your Galaxy's Screen on Another Display with SideSync

- Samsung has created a new, free software tool called SideSync, which lets you mirror your Galaxy's display on a computer screen or an Android tablet's screen.

- To use SideSync, you need to download it from the Google Play Store. Additionally, you need to install SideSync on the partner device.
- If the partner device is an Android tablet, download SideSync from the Google Play Store the same way you did on your S7 or S7 Edge.
- If the partner device is a PC or Mac, download SideSync from the following URL.

http://www.samsung.com/us/sidesync/

- Once SideSync is installed on the partner device, start SideSync on both devices and follow the instructions provided.
- While SideSync claims to be able to connect to your computer via Wi-Fi, I found wireless connectivity to be flaky, whereas USB was very reliable. I recommend using USB if mirroring your display on your Mac or PC.

Disabling Annoying Sounds and Vibrations

- By default, TouchWiz makes a lot of blips and bloops. For those of us who relish peace and quiet, it's easy to disable them.
- Go to system settings → "Sounds and vibration." Disable some or all of the following:
  - o   Touch sounds

- o Screen lock sounds
- o Charging sound
- o Dialing keypad tone
- o Keyboard sound

- Personally, I also change my default notification sound from "Whisper" to "Beep Once" (Tap "Notification sound" → "Default notification sound" → "Beep Once"). I find "Beep Once" more professional and less intrusive than the default notification sound.

Customizing the Notification Panel Toggle Buttons

- Customize the toggle buttons displayed in the notification panel by swiping down the notification panel with two fingers and tapping "Edit."
- Tap, hold, and drag the toggle buttons to rearrange them.
- Releasing a toggle button over another toggle button on this screen causes the two toggle buttons to swap places.
- Note that only the first 10 toggle buttons, highlighted in light blue, are available in the notification panel. Swipe the toggle buttons in the notification panel right to see toggles 6-10.

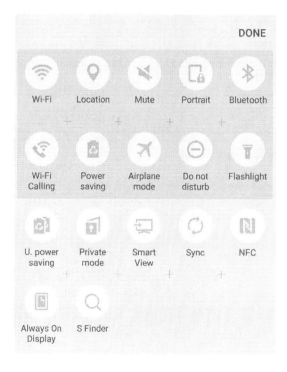

- Be sure to tap "Done" when finished, or your changes will not be saved.

Vision Accessibility Settings for Users Hard of Seeing

- Voice Assistant is the main feature of the S7 / S7 Edge for users who are hard of seeing. Enable it in system settings → "Accessibility" → "Vision" → "Voice Assistant."
- When it is enabled, the entire TouchWiz experience changes. To use the device with Voice Assistant enabled, drag your finger around the display to make the device select different elements and speak a description of them to you. For example, it highlights buttons, menu items, and so on.
- Once you have successfully selected a screen element, double-tap anywhere on the screen to activate it (equivalent to a single tap under normal circumstances).
- Scrolling is accomplished by swiping with two fingers at once.
- Similarly, pull down the notification panel by using two fingers.
- The S7 / S7 Edge have several other vision accessibility settings. From system settings → "Accessibility" → "Vision," you can also adjust the system font size, magnification gestures, colors, and more.

Zooming in on Any Screen

- Your Galaxy has a very cool zoom feature that allows you to triple tap on any screen to zoom in.
- Enable it in system settings → "Accessibility" → "Vision" → "Magnification gestures."
- Triple-tap anywhere to zoom in, and then pan using two fingers.
- You can also triple-tap and hold the third tap to temporarily zoom in.

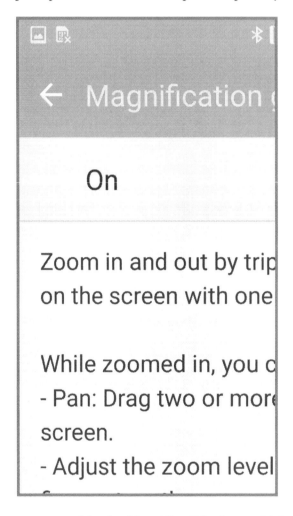

- Alternatively, you can enable the Magnifier Window, which provides a loupe-like window you can move around the screen:

- Enable the Magnifier Window in system settings → "Accessibility" → "Vision" → "Magnifier window."

Improving Font Contrast

- If you find it difficult to read some of the white and light gray fonts used throughout TouchWiz, try enabling "High contrast fonts" in system settings → "Accessibility" → "Vision."

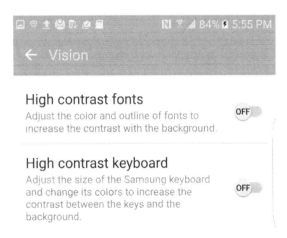

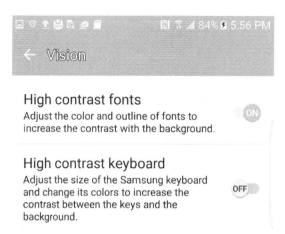

High contrast fonts

Adjust the color and outline of fonts to increase the contrast with the background.

High contrast keyboard

Adjust the size of the Samsung keyboard and change its colors to increase the contrast between the keys and the background.

Improving Keyboard Contrast

- Right below the "High contrast fonts" setting is a "High contrast keyboard" setting, which works similarly, although with somewhat garish colors.

Blocking Unwanted Calls

- To block a number from calling you, open a call from that number in the "Logs" tab of the Phone app and tap "More" → "Block/unblock number." Then enable or disable call and message blocking.

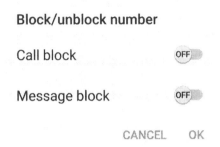

- To manage your reject list or to block a number you haven't already received a call from, open the Phone app and tap "More" → "Settings" → "Call blocking" → "Block list."

Configuring Hands-Free Options and Voice Commands

- The S7 / S7 Edge have a number of hands-free options that are useful if you drive a lot or otherwise have your hands full.

Answering Calls Easily with the Home Button

- This is a cool feature that makes it easier to answer phone calls that you *do* want. Open the Phone app and go to "More" → "Settings" → Answering and ending calls" and enable "Pressing the Home key."

Going Hands-Free with Car Mode

- Car Mode is a special hands-free mode optimized for driving.
- It gives you a simplified home screen containing only options for placing calls, sending text messages, starting navigation, and playing music.
- Better yet, you can use all the features of Car Mode with your voice. It looks like this:

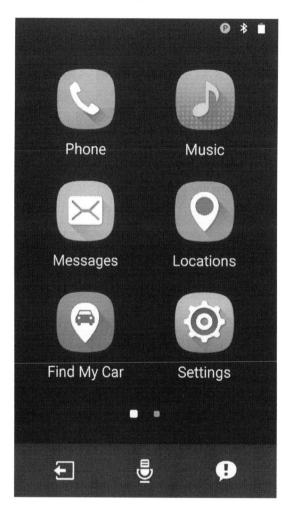

- To use Car Mode, download and install Car Mode from the "Galaxy Apps" store in your app drawer. After you've installed Car Mode, it appears in your app drawer as well.

- The first time you enter Car Mode, you have to accept several legal disclaimers and configure a wake-up command if you have not already done so. Just follow the prompts and answer the questions you are asked. If your car stereo supports Bluetooth, follow the instructions to pair your Galaxy with your car.

- Once you've configured Car Mode and you see the main screen, just say your wake-up command out loud, wait for the tone, and then speak a command. For example:
  - o "Call John on mobile."
  - o "Send a text message to Mike."
  - o "Play Daft Punk."
  - o "Navigate to Target."

- When you receive an incoming call in Car Mode, say "Accept" or "Reject' out loud to answer or decline the call.

- Tap 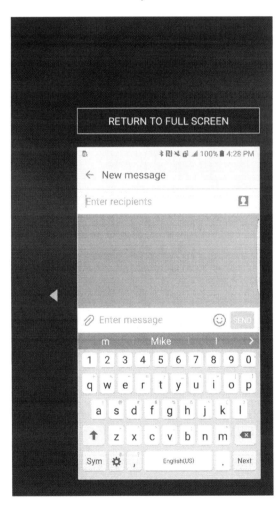 to exit Car Mode.

Shrinking the Screen for One-Handed Operation

- The S7 and S7 Edge have a convenient one-handed mode that shrinks down the screen to make it more thumb-friendly:

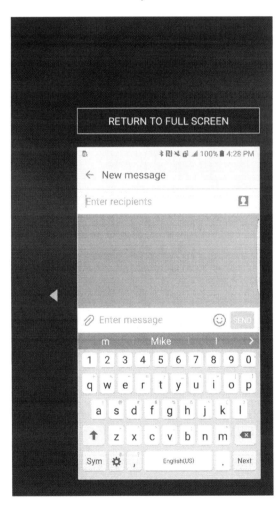

- To enable this mode, go to system settings → "Advanced features" → "One-handed operation" and turn on "Reduce screen size."
- Then, triple-press ⬭ to enter or exit one-handed operation at any time.
- If you'd like to shrink the Samsung keyboard only, enable "One-handed input" in system settings → "Advanced features" → "One-handed operation." Note that this mode doesn't have a quick-access shortcut like triple tapping ⬭. It can only be enabled or disabled from this menu.

Enabling the Assistant Menu for Easier Button Access

- The Assistant Menu is a movable button (tap, hold, and drag) that provides easy access to common shortcuts such as home, back, recent apps, volume, lock screen, screen capture, and much more.

- Enable it in system settings → "Accessibility" → "Dexterity and interaction" → "Assistant menu."

- Be sure to investigate all the settings available for the Assistant Menu, including Assistant Plus, which adds app-specific shortcuts to the Assistant Menu.

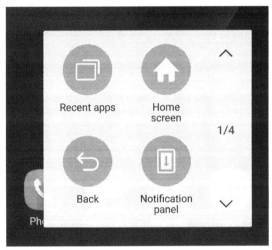

Configuring Motion Shortcuts

- The S7 / S7 Edge support some useful motion controls like automatically calling an on-screen contact by raising the device to your ear (Direct Call), or silencing it by placing it face down on a surface (Easy Mute).
- To enable these and other motions, go to system settings → "Advanced features."

Keeping the Screen On by Monitoring Your Face

- The S7 / S7 Edge have an experimental feature called Smart Stay that uses the front camera to observe your face and keep the screen on as long as you're looking at it. I think this feature is a curiosity more than anything else, but it's still interesting to try out, and may be a sign of things to come in future devices.
- Turn it on in system settings → "Display" → "Smart stay."

Tapping to Pay with Samsung Pay

- Samsung Pay is one of the S7 / S7 Edge's main selling points, and is one of my favorite features.

- What is Samsung Pay? It's a digital wallet that lets you register your debit/credit cards so you can pay at retail locations with your S7 / S7 Edge. Of course, tap-to-pay is nothing new. Both Androids and iPhones have supported tap-to-pay for a couple years now through apps such as Google Wallet and Apple Pay. The key innovation in Samsung Pay is its built-in LoopPay technology, which lets you wirelessly trigger any magnetic swipe terminal just by holding your Galaxy next to it.

- That's right—with Samsung Pay, you can use your Galaxy to pay at ANY credit/debit card terminal that takes a card swipe—not just the NFC tap-to-pay terminals found in gas stations, Walgreens, and McDonalds. Pretty sweet! I've been using Samsung Pay since is debuted on the Note 5 in 2015, and it's saved me a couple times when I got to the cash register and realized I'd forgotten my wallet.

> **TIP:** *New Samsung Pay users are eligible for a $30 gift card between 3/11/16 and 3/31/16. Check here (p. 237) for details.*

Setting up Samsung Pay

- Find the Samsung Pay app in your app drawer (Verizon users: Samsung Pay doesn't come preinstalled on your S7. Download it from the Google Play Store instead).

- Tap it, and then tap "Install" to download the necessary software components. Tap "Install" again when prompted, to confirm the installation.

Tap Install to download and install
Samsung Pay.

File size : 28 MB

INSTALL

- You see a short intro video demonstrating Samsung Pay, and then you're prompted to sign into your Samsung account if you haven't already done so. You can't use Samsung Pay without signing into, so sign in.

Samsung account

aaronh123987@gmail.com

•••••••••

Forgot your ID or password?

I am a new user.
Sign up

CANCEL   SIGN IN

- Once signed in, tap "Start" and follow the prompts to agree to the terms of service and register a fingerprint and PIN.
- Finally, tap "Add card" to begin registering your debit or credit card.

- Follow the prompts to finish registering your card using your Galaxy's camera. Your Galaxy uses its rear camera to automatically read your cardholder name, number, and date of expiration.
- After successful registration, a new "Simple Pay" tab appears at the bottom of your home screen:

Paying with Samsung Pay

- To make a payment using the card you've added, swipe up the Samsung Pay "Simple Pay" tab at the bottom of your home screen.

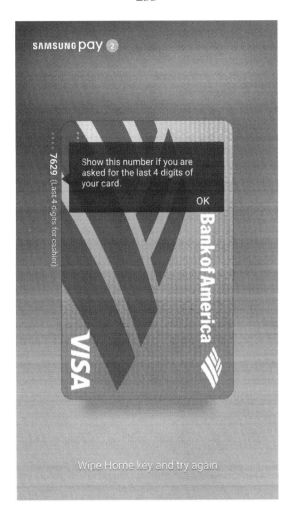

- When you see your card, press and hold your finger on 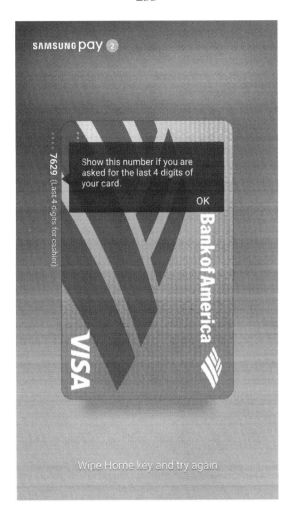 to verify your fingerprint.
- Then, hold your Galaxy within a couple inches of the card terminal. Your Galaxy automatically detects the optimal method of payment (NFC or magnetic), and you receive a notification when the payment is complete.
- If you are required to provide the last 4 digits of your card, use the one-time number provided to the left of your card image (see above screenshot). That's all there is to it!

Limitations and Supported Banks

- Note that Samsung Pay does not work with every time of magnetic terminal. In particular, it doesn't work with "dip" terminals where you insert your card instead of swiping it. Occasionally, you may also find that it fails with some swipe terminals, although this is rare.

- Check the following link for details about supported banks:

> *http://www.samsung.com/us/support/answer/ANS00043884/9974088
> 20/Y/*
>
> *(Short URL: http://goo.gl/Uete6F)*

TIP: *Samsung Pay is much more secure than a traditional credit card payment. It masks your real credit card number when you make a payment. The merchant never sees or records your credit card number—only a one-time "token" that authorizes the transaction and then becomes useless. This is a really great side benefit of using tap-to-pay payment systems that a lot of people don't realize! When you use Samsung Pay, you protect yourself from card skimmers and other unscrupulous schemes.*

Downloading Files Super-Fast with Download Booster

- Download Booster combines your Wi-Fi and 4G LTE connections to download files larger than 30 MB super-fast.
- To use Download Booster, go to system settings → "More connection settings" → "Download booster" and turn the slider on.
- When you are in range of both Wi-Fi and 4G LTE and you're downloading a file larger than 30 MB, Download Booster kicks in:

- Download Booster only works with file downloads in the Internet browser, Chrome, YouTube, the Play Store, and a select few other apps. If you try to use it with a third-party app, it may not work.
- If you have a limited data plan, keep an eye on your usage or consider setting download limits to avoid expensive overage charges.

Using Quick Connect Mode to Share Media with Nearby Devices

- The Galaxy S line has slowly but steadily accumulated a vast selection of media sharing modes. If you've owned a Samsung phone before, you probably remember things like Group Play, AllShare Cast, DLNA, and other vaguely named media sharing tools.
- Well, Samsung finally realized that these options had gotten out of control and no one understood what they were for or how to use them. So, they consolidated all of these features into Quick Connect Mode.
- Quick Connect mode allows your Galaxy to connect and share media with other nearby Galaxy devices, smart TVs, game consoles, video dongles, Galaxy Gear smart watches, and so on. For compatible media devices, Quick Connect guides you through the process and makes it easy to share your photos, videos, or other files.
- Access Quick Connect mode by swiping down the notification panel and tapping "Quick Connect."

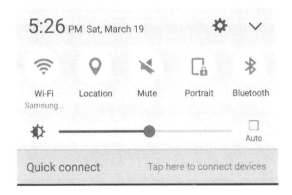

- Your Galaxy automatically detects nearby media devices and tells you what media sharing actions you can take with each device.
- To get started, just tap a device and follow the prompts. You may need to put other devices in their "sharing" or "discoverable" modes for your Galaxy to detect and connect to them.

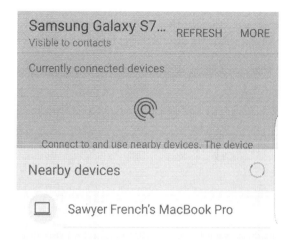

Searching Your Galaxy Using S Finder

- S Finder is a search engine that searches (almost) all the data on your Galaxy.
- Let's say you want to find everything pertaining to your friend Mike Lee. Without S Finder, you would have to open each app individually to search for information. For example, searching for "Mike Lee" in the Phone app would turn up Mike's contact information but not any text messages or e-mails in which he participated. S Finder solves this problem by providing a centralized search function for multiple apps.
- S Finder has one major limitation: it doesn't support searching your Gmail inbox. And of course, there's no guarantee it'll work with data from third-party apps. But for searching through stock apps, it's quite effective.
- Access S Finder by swiping down the notification panel with two fingers and tapping "S Finder."

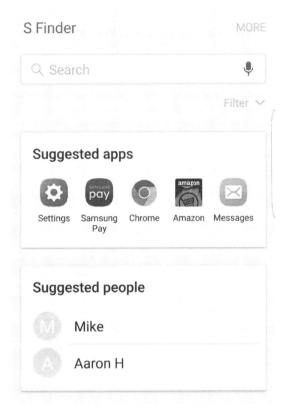

Claiming Your Free Gifts from Samsung

- For past Galaxy S launches, Samsung partnered with companies like Dropbox, Evernote, and The Wall Street Journal to give away free software and subscriptions with every Galaxy S. Samsung hasn't facilitated the same offer for Galaxy S7 buyers. However, there are several other freebies this time that are arguably even better.
    - **Free Gear VR with $50 worth of free games:** If you pre-ordered or bought your S7 between 2/23/16 and 3/18/2016, you are entitled to a free Gear VR, Samsung's virtual reality headset, a $100 value. Redeem at https://promos.samsungpromotions.com/GearVR Additionally, once you've received your Gear VR and installed the Oculus app as per its instructions, you will receive six games worth $50 in the "Download" section of the Oculus app.
    - **Free Year of Netflix:** If you pre-ordered or bought your S7 between 2/23/16 and 3/18/2016, you are entitled to a free year of Netflix, a $96 value. Redeem at https://promos.samsungpromotions.com/GearVR
    - **$30 Gift Card for New Samsung Pay Users:** If you're a new Samsung Pay user, just add a card and make your first payment between 3/11/16 and 3/31/16 and you'll receive an on-phone popup message to claim a $30 gift

card to Regal Theaters, Nike, eBay, Whole Foods, or Best Buy. See offer details at: http://www.samsung.com/us/samsung-pay/

Keeping Your Device Awake While Charging

- The longest available screen timeout setting on the S7 / S7 Edge is 10 minutes. Sometimes this isn't enough. For example, when I'm using a calculator app on my phone, I don't want it to sleep at all.

- Fortunately, there's a way to accomplish this. Go to system settings → "About device." Swipe down until you see "Build number." Repeatedly tap this box. A message appears stating that you are about to become a developer. Keep going until Developer Mode is activated.

- Now, tap ⤺ . A new option appears in system settings called "Developer options." Tap this, and then enable "Stay awake." Done! As long as your device is plugged in and charging, it won't go to sleep.

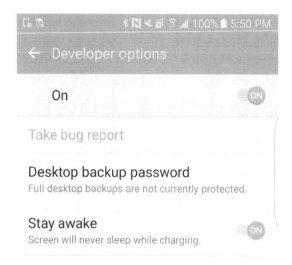

Taking Screenshots

- Want to take screenshots like the ones included in this book? Just press and hold the ⬭ and power buttons together for approximately one second until the screen flashes.

- Or, place the side of your hand flat against one side of the screen and swipe the opposite direction.

- Your screenshot is saved in your Gallery with the rest of your photos.

Maintaining Peace of Mind with Do Not Disturb Mode

- Do Not Disturb mode lets you set quiet hours during which your Galaxy will not display or sound notifications.
- Access it by going to system settings → "Sounds and vibration" → "Do not disturb." Enable it by tapping "Turn on now." Note that "Turn on now" turns on Do Not Disturb mode until you manually switch it off again.
- To schedule Do Not Disturb mode so it kicks in automatically during a set time only, enable "Turn on as scheduled" and specify a schedule using the "Days," "Start time," and "End time" options.
- To selectively block notifications, either by notification type or by contact, tap "Allow exceptions." You can selectively block calls, notifications, alarms, text messages, events and reminders, or any combination of those things. Tap "Calls from" or "Messages from" to set exceptions by contact (for example, your spouse or kids).

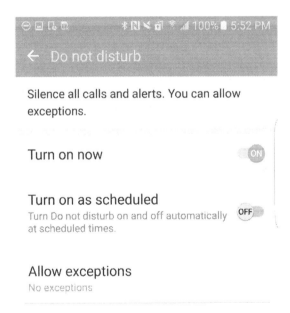

Conserving Battery Power with Power Saving Modes

- The S7 / S7 Edge have two power saving modes: regular Power Saving Mode and Ultra Power Saving Mode.
- Regular Power Saving Mode works by dimming the screen, restricting CPU performance, shutting off the touch key backlights, and making a few other adjustments. Turn it on by swiping down the notification panel, swiping the toggles to the right, and enabling "Power saving."

- Ultra Power Saving Mode takes things even further. In addition to forcing grayscale mode, dimming the backlight, and restricting CPU performance, it deactivates Wi-Fi and Bluetooth, deactivates mobile data while the screen is off, and limits you to a few select apps.

- You only want to use Ultra Power Saving Mode when you absolutely need to conserve your battery power down to the last drop. It's similar to the power conservation features of Emergency Mode (p. 260) but without the safety features.

- Turn it on by swiping down the notification panel with two fingers and enabling "U. power saving."

Accessing Kids Mode

- Kids Mode sets up a "sandbox" environment for young kids. It contains various fun apps and games that entertain your kids without letting them screw up your phone.

- You must download Kids Mode before you can use it. To do so, go to your app drawer and open the Galaxy Apps store. Search for and download Kids Mode and follow the prompts to install the app.

- After installation, the Kids Mode app appears in your app drawer. Tap it to launch Kids Mode.

- When you first launch Kids Mode, you need to set a PIN used for disabling Kids Mode in the future and enter your child's name and date of birth. You are also prompted to select which, if any, third-party apps and contacts are allowed in Kids Mode.

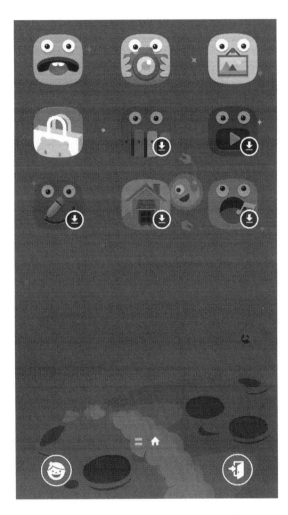

- The two buttons at the bottom of the screen open parental control and close Kids Mode, respectively.
- If you forget your PIN code while Kids Mode is engaged, you must remove the battery from your Galaxy to exit Kids Mode.

Using Your Galaxy as a Magnifying Glass

- Your Galaxy comes with a widget that lets you use the camera and flash LED as an illuminated magnifying lens, and the feature works quite well.
- To use it, go to the home screen and add a widget (p. 73). Swipe right to the Magnifier widget, and tap and hold it to add it.

- After placing the Magnifier widget on a home screen, just tap to launch it.

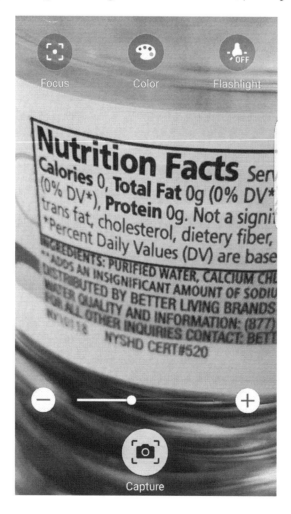

- Tap anywhere on the screen or tap the "Focus" button to autofocus the image. If the camera refuses to focus, increase the distance between your Galaxy and the object you are trying to focus on.

- Adjust the zoom level with the slider on the bottom of the screen or by pinching in and out, and turn on illumination and/or capture a photograph using the buttons on the screen.

S Health: Managing Your Diet, Exercise, and Fitness

- S Health is Samsung's entry into the growing mobile health & fitness market. It's an app designed to help you track all aspects of your exercise and diet and is compatible with a huge selection of fitness accessories like the Samsung Gear Fit, various Fitbit devices, and more.

- In my opinion, if your goal is to get into shape or lose weight, you should consult a professional or at least do your own research instead of completely relying on an app made by Samsung. Safely and effectively improving your health and fitness requires knowledge, not just a smartphone app. However, S Health is a fine assistant if you're only interested in tracking calories and basic health stats as part of a broader fitness program. S Health is not really a "coach"—instead, think of it as a very high-tech logbook.

- The first time you open S Health, you have to consent to the terms of use. You also see a message asking you to sync S Health with your Samsung account, if you're logged into one. Tap "Setup" and enable auto sync. You want your fitness data to be backed up to the cloud so you don't lose it if you lose your Galaxy.

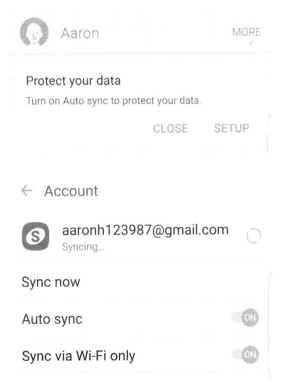

- The main S Health screen looks like this:

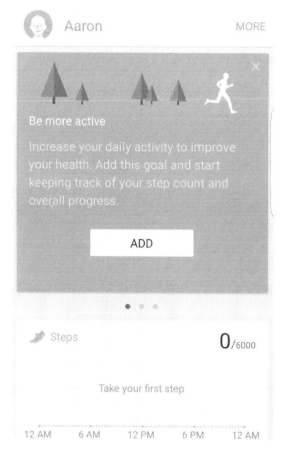

- First, tap → "Profile" to customize your profile, including gender, age, weight, height, etc. S Health requires this information to perform accurately interpret fitness data like steps taken, calories, etc.
- After you've set up your profile, return to the main S Health screen and scroll down to view more tiles. Tiles are the main engine of S Health. Use them to record and monitor all your health data.

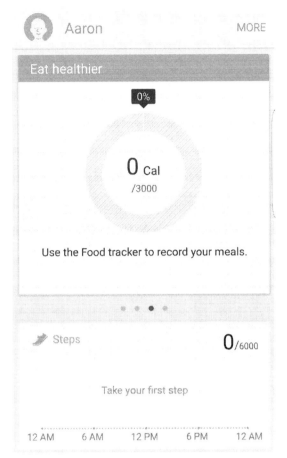

Aaron   MORE

Eat healthier

0%

0 Cal
/3000

Use the Food tracker to record your meals.

• • • • •

🏃 Steps   0/6000

Take your first step

12 AM   6 AM   12 PM   6 PM   12 AM

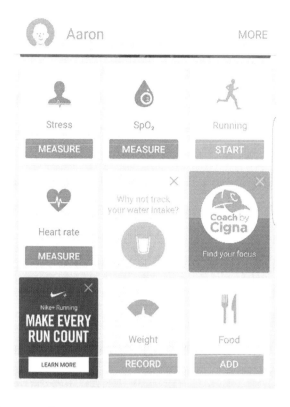

- Tap a tile to input and track data. To add or remove tiles, tap "More" → "Manage items." Available tiles include:

Trackers

- Steps (pedometer; works even while S Health is closed and the device is asleep)
- Walking
- Running
- Cycling
- Hiking
- Sports
- Food
- Water
- Caffeine
- Weight
- Sleep
- Heart rate
- SpO2 (oxygen level)
- Stress
- Blood glucose

- Blood pressure

Goals

- Be more active
- Eat healthier
- Feel more rested

Programs

- Baby steps to 5K
- Run 5K
- First attempt at 10K
- Run 10K

- Overall, the key to using S Health is to be diligent in inputting information into tiles. The more data S Health gathers about you, the better it can help you manage your goals and help you understand the progression of your fitness over time.

- In my opinion, S Health's main strength is its ability to store your health data and visually display it with logs and charts. S Health's running programs and goals are less compelling; you're probably better off doing your own research when setting fitness goals. But for tracking information while pursuing your goals, S Health excels.

Measuring Your Heart Rate

- To take a quick heart rate measurement, enable the "Heart rate" tile in "More" → "Manage items" → "Trackers" and tap "Measure" on the Heart rate tile.
- Place the tip of your index finger lightly on the sensor next to the rear camera lens. Hold still until your heart rate has been successfully measured.
- If the measurement fails, you were probably pressing too hard. Try again with the tip of your finger softly resting on the sensor.

Tracking Your Steps with the Pedometer

- S Health's built-in pedometer (the large "Steps" tile) tracks your steps even when S Health is not running and your Galaxy is asleep.
- No setup is necessary; after you've launched S Health for the first time, the pedometer automatically starts tracking your steps.

- You can optionally set a step target by tapping the Steps tile, then "More" → "Set target," but this isn't necessary to simply track your steps.
- Return to the "Steps" tile at any time to view your count.

Connecting Compatible Accessories

- If you have a companion device (e.g., a running watch) that's compatible with S Health, you can configure it to wirelessly sync its data with S Health.
- To view a list of compatible accessories, go to the main S Health screen and tap "More" → "Accessories." To connect an accessory, tap its name in the "Accessories" list and then tap "Register" to begin the pairing process.

Printing with Google Cloud Print

- Google Cloud Print is a utility from Google that makes it easy to wirelessly print documents from your Galaxy.
- First, you need to set up your printer with Google Cloud Print. On your desktop computer, go to the link below.
- If your printer connects to your computer via USB, click the "Add Classic Printer" button and follow the instructions. If your printer has Wi-Fi or is connected to the Internet via an Ethernet cable, click the "Add Cloud Ready Printer" button instead.

---

http://www.google.com/landing/cloudprint/

- After your printer is configured, open the Google Play Store on your Galaxy and search for "Cloud Print." Download and install the app.
- Once installed, you receive a notification in your notification panel. Tap it to enable the Cloud Print service. If you don't see the notification, instead go to system settings → "More connection settings" → "Printing" → "Cloud Print" and enable Cloud Print.
- If you've already set up your printer using your computer, its name appears on this screen. This means you're ready to print.

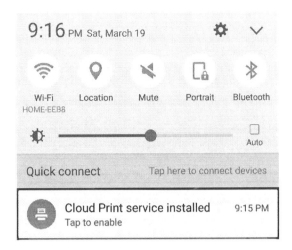

- Now, in any app that has a print function (like Microsoft Office (p. 182)), you're able to wirelessly print using your printer via Cloud Print.

- Additionally, you can print anything that you can share with the Share Via (p. 94) tool. To do so, tap "Print" on the Share Via (p. 94) screen → 🖨.

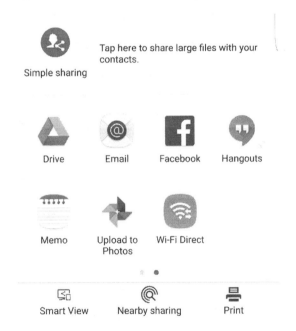

Disabling Briefing to Speed Up Your Galaxy

- The S7 / S7 Edge come preloaded with Briefing, a social media and news aggregator app accessed by swiping left from the main home screen. Briefing is pretty, but it's not as functional as many 3rd party apps like GReader (p. 301) and Pulse from the Google Play Store. Plus, it's too easy to accidentally start Briefing by accident.

- If you don't use Briefing, disable it to avoid accidental launches and to slightly speed up your device. Tap  to go to the home screen, and then tap and hold an empty space on the home screen to open the home screen menu. Swipe left to the Briefing page and change the slider to "Off."

Taking Advantage of Cloud Storage with Google Drive

- This tip not only powers up your Galaxy, but also your computing in general. In fact, it's one of my top tech tips of all time.
- What is cloud storage? It's hard disk space that's on a remote server instead of your computer's internal hard drive. Common cloud storage services include Dropbox, Google Drive, OneDrive, and more. When you install a cloud storage utility on your computer, it creates a new folder that works like any other folder, except the files you save in it are automatically and instantaneously backed up to the remote server I mentioned.

What are the advantages?

- If your computer crashes or is lost or stolen, any files saved to your cloud storage folder are **safely backed up** to the cloud. You won't lose your data.

- You can install a cloud storage utility on multiple computers to easily **synchronize your files** between them. Say you install a cloud storage utility on both your home and work computers. Any time you save a file to the cloud storage folder on your home computer, it is instantly synchronized to your work computer—and vice versa. No more need to carry USB drives back and forth.

- **Every version of every file is backed up.** Did you accidentally corrupt a document and save over it? No problem—you can easily roll back to a previous version.

- If you need a file while you're away from your computer, you can login to the service's website and **download** the necessary file with an Internet browser.

- If you **upgrade your computer**, you won't have to worry about transferring your data. Just install the cloud storage utility on your new computer, and it automatically downloads all your files to your new hard drive.

- Finally, every major cloud storage service offers an **Android app**, so you can access your files from your Galaxy on-the-go. In conjunction with apps like Microsoft Office (p. 182), you can easily view and edit your documents from your device.

- Personally, I keep all of my work and personal files in my cloud storage folder, and I suggest you do, too. It makes life a lot easier, and at some point, is guaranteed to save you from disaster.

- I used to use Dropbox because it was more polished than Google Drive, but now I recommend Google Drive. Drive gives you more free storage space than Dropbox (15 GB vs. 2 GB), has more affordable paid tiers (100 GB for $1.99/month), and integrates nicely with Gmail and other Google services. To get started, download the desktop utility from the following link and download the Android app from the Google Play Store.

https://www.google.com/drive/download/

Detecting Crying Babies and Ringing Doorbells

- Here's a weird one: a feature to detect crying babies or ringing doorbells. I know, it's a bit…oddly specific, and of questionable usefulness. But if, say, your job requires you to work from home and wear headphones all day, maybe you'll find it useful?
- Go to system settings → "Accessibility" → "Hearing" → "Sound detectors." The doorbell detector requires you to record samples of your doorbell ringing before you can use it, but the baby crying detector does not.

Changing the System Font

- Want to personalize your Galaxy with a custom font? Go to system settings → "Display" → "Font." A custom font applies to all system menus, the home screen, the app drawer, most apps, and more.

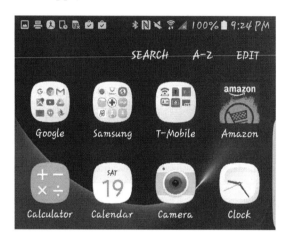

Disabling Useless Apps for Good

- Ever heard the term "bloatware?" It refers to preloaded software that you don't want. Although the S7 and S7 Edge don't have as much bloatware as some older Samsung phones have had (Galaxy S4, I'm looking at you), there are some apps that you might not want on your device, like Samsung Milk Music and Facebook.
- You can't completely uninstall these apps since they're in the device's ROM (read-only memory), but you can disable them so they don't appear in your app drawer and consume system resources. To do so, go to the app drawer and tap "Edit." Tap the red minus sign on any app you want to disable and confirm when prompted. Tap "Done" to exit this mode.

Using the Camera Flash as a Flashlight

- Your Galaxy has a built-in toggle button that lets you use the camera's LED flash as a flashlight. Use this feature by swiping down the notification panel, swiping the toggle buttons right, and enabling "Flashlight."

⭐ **TIP:** *Try the TeslaLED (p. 308) app for a brighter flashlight, plus additional options like a strobe and Morse code. You can't place TeslaLED in your toggle buttons like you can with Flashlight, but it does come with widgets (p. 68) you can place on your home screen.*

Speeding Up the Home Button by Disabling Camera Quick Launch

- By default, double-tapping ⬭ launches the Camera app (in about 0.7 seconds!). This means that whenever you tap the ⬭ button once to go to the home screen, there is a slight delay while the system waits for a second press. If you don't care about launching the camera with the home button, you can turn off this shortcut and make single presses of the home button register faster.

- To do so, open the Camera app and tap ◄ → ⚙. Disable "Quick launch." You'll notice the home button is snappier with this setting disabled.

- Personally, I think the slight sluggishness is worth the convenience of being able to open the Camera app so quickly; it lets me get a lot more shots I would otherwise miss.

Getting 4 Hours of Juice in 10 Minutes with Adaptive Fast Charging

- The S7 / S7 Edge have a new feature called Adaptive Fast Charging that lets you charge your battery faster than ever before. Samsung claims that your Galaxy can operate for up to 4 hours after just 10 minutes of charging.

- To take advantage of Adaptive Fast Charging, just make sure you're using the power brick and USB cord that came with your device, plugged into a regular AC outlet. Adaptive Fast Charging won't work if you use a different power brick or a USB port. Additionally, it may not kick in if you use a third-party USB cord that is not of sufficient wire gauge (so stick to the white Samsung cord that comes with the S7).

- Make sure the device's screen is turned off to charge as quickly as possible.

> *TIP: Any third party charging accessory that conforms to the Quick Charge 2.0 standard are compatible with Adaptive Fast Charging. Look for this designation when buying aftermarket chargers.*

Troubleshooting Apps by Clearing App Cache and Data

- If one of your apps is acting buggy, the first line of defense is restarting your Galaxy by pressing and holding the power button, then "Restart."

- If restarting doesn't fix the problem, though, the next step is clearing app and cache data. Go to system settings → "Applications" → "Application manager." Scroll down and tap on the app that's misbehaving. Tap "Storage," then "Clear cache" and "Clear data."

- This resets the app to its original state. In general, this doesn't delete user data like notes, contacts, or pictures—just temporary settings and configuration information.

> *TIP: Having a network-related problem? Try clearing all network settings in system settings → "Backup and reset" → "Reset network settings."*

Keeping Things Running Smoothly with Auto Restart

- The S7 / S7 Edge have a new feature to help you keep your device running smoothly at all times—Auto Restart. This feature lets you schedule regular device restarts so everything is always nice and fresh. I strongly recommend enabling this feature, because regularly restarting your Android is one of the best ways to prevent buggy behavior.

- To set up Auto Restart, go to system settings → "Backup and reset" → "Auto restart." Note that this feature may not be available if you have a carrier-branded phone—it's generally only enabled on unlocked and international devices.

Setting Up Blackberry-Like Text Shortcuts

- How many of us used Blackberries before Android hit the scene? Blackberries had a lot of very cool keyboard shortcuts and tricks to master. Samsung has included one very Blackberry-like feature in the Samsung keyboard: Text Shortcuts.

- With Text Shortcuts, you can program your Galaxy to automatically convert abbreviations into longer words or phrases. For example, you can program it to change "bc" to "because," "wrt" to "with regards to," or "em" to your email address. Text Shortcuts can save a lot of typing for your most-used words or phrases.

- To enable Text Shortcuts, go to system settings → "Language and input" → "Samsung keyboard" → "Text shortcuts."

Powering Up Your Selfies with Wide-Angle Group Shots

- If you're not already familiar with the term "selfie," it refers to a self-shot portrait. Almost all newer smartphones have a front camera specifically for taking selfies, but the S7 / S7 Edge have a special feature for group selfies. It's called wide-angle selfie mode, which is basically a panorama mode for the front camera, allowing you to capture more people in a group.

- To use it, open the camera app and tap to switch to front camera mode. Then, tap "Mode" → "Wide selfie" and follow the instructions.

Customizing Quick Settings to Speed Up Settings Access

- The S7 / S7 Edge's settings menu is long and not particularly easy to navigate. If you find yourself always scrolling around the page in search of a particular category, consider adding it to your Quick Settings.

- To do so, go to system settings → "Edit." Place a checkmark next to your most frequently used settings pages to pin them to the top of the settings page for easier access.

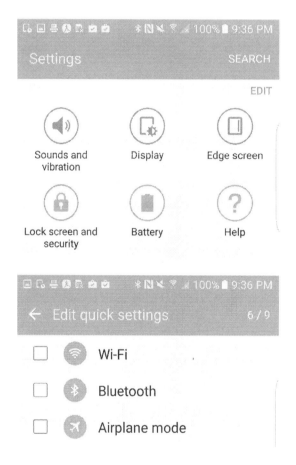

Pinpointing Battery Drain

- Normal battery use is <1% per hour while asleep (thanks to Android 6.0 Marshmallow's new Doze feature) and around 10% or more per hour while awake, depending on what task you're doing.

- If your Galaxy is consuming significantly more battery power than this, you might have a rogue app that's sucking down your juice. To pinpoint the source of the drain, go to system settings → "Battery" → "Battery usage" and look for any apps that are consuming a significant percentage of battery power. Uninstall or disable (p. 252) these apps.

> ⭐ **TIP:** If nothing looks out of the ordinary in the Battery settings but you're still experiencing drain, try installing BetterBatteryStats from the Google Play Store. This app examines battery drain at a much deeper level and is useful for particularly tricky sources of battery drain. Search Google for more information on using BetterBatteryStats.

Waking Up Your Galaxy with the Wave of a Hand

- The "Easy screen turn on" feature lets you wake your Galaxy by waving your hand over it instead of pressing the power button. This feature uses a sensor next to the front camera, so the device must be screen-up for it to work.
- To enable it, go to system settings → "Accessibility" → "Dexterity and interaction" → "Easy screen turn on."

All About Notifications

Never Miss a Notification with Smart Alert

- How often do you pick up your phone throughout the day to check the LED light for notifications? I know I do it all the time. The S7 / S7 Edge have a special feature that makes your device vibrate when you pick it up and there are new notifications. This helps ensure you don't miss any notifications as you check throughout the day.
- To turn Smart Alert on, go to system settings → "Advanced features" and enable "Smart alert."

Using the Camera Flash for Notifications

- The iPhone has offered flash notifications for a while, and Android has only recently caught up. With flash notifications, your camera flash blinks to provide a more visible signal than the usual dim LED. Of course, remember that you'll only be able to see the flash blink if the device is face down.
- To enable this feature, go to system settings → "Accessibility" → "Hearing" and enable "Flash notification."

Getting Repeat Reminders for Missed Notifications

- By default, notifications make a sound the first time they appear in your notification panel, but never again.
- If you want to receipt repeat reminders (e.g., every 5 minutes) for unacknowledged notifications, go to system settings → "Accessibility" → "Notification reminder."

Configuring Lock Screen Notifications and App-Specific Notifications

- The S7 and S7 Edge have some new notification control settings.
- First, you can control if and how notifications are shown on your lock screen in system settings → "Lock screen and security" → "Notifications on lock screen" (only visible if you have a lock screen enabled).
    - o "Show content" shows all notifications while your device is locked.
    - o "Hide content" still shows all notifications, but hide sensitive details like the actual text of text messages or the contents of email.
    - o "Do not show notifications" prevents your device from displaying any notifications at all on your lock screen.
- Second, you can tailor notifications on a per-app basis. You can block all notifications, set an app's notifications as priority so they always appear at the top of your notification panel, choose whether to hide that app's notifications on the lock screen, and more.
- Find these options in system settings → "Notifications." Tap "Advanced" and then an app's name to access detailed settings.

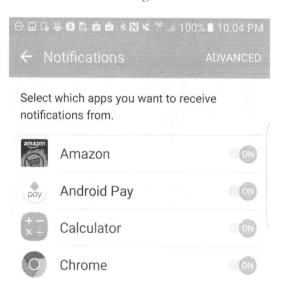

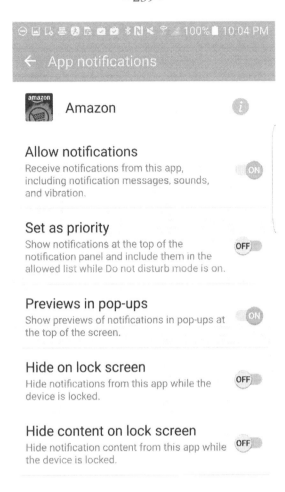

Connecting Your Galaxy to Your Car Using MirrorLink

- MirrorLink is a new feature for connecting your Android device to a MirrorLink-enabled vehicle. It allows you to control your phone and access its apps and media using your car's infotainment system (i.e., its dashboard/steering wheel buttons).

- Today, pretty much every vehicle and car stereo manufacturer has a different protocol for interfacing with your phone; sure, they all use Bluetooth, but the details are very different. MirrorLink aims to standardize this process and provide new functionality, like accessing your Maps app with your car's controls.

- If your car supports MirrorLink, it automatically detects your S7 / S7 Edge when you plug it in via USB. If it doesn't immediately detect your device, make sure that MirrorLink is enabled in system settings → "More connection settings" → "MirrorLink."

- Consult your car's instruction manual for details on operating your Galaxy with the car's built-in controls.

Simplifying Gestures with Single Tap Mode

- Single tap mode changes several tap-and-drag gestures to single taps, including dismissing alarms & events and answering and rejecting calls.
- Enable it in system settings → "Accessibility."

Configuring SOS Messages and Using Emergency Mode

- The S7 / S7 Edge have a mode called Emergency Mode, which disables all non-essential features, extends battery life as much as possible, and gives you a simplified control panel.
- Turn it on by pressing and holding the power button, then tapping "Emergency mode." Use it if you're in a bad situation and you need your battery to last as long as possible, or if you just need easy access to a flashlight and an alarm.
- You can also configure an SOS message, which can be dispatched at any time by triple-pressing the power button.
- To configure an SOS message, go to system settings → "Privacy and safety" → "Send SOS messages." Switch this feature on and configure settings as desired.
- Now, any time you triple-press the power button—even with the device asleep and locked—it takes pictures with the front and back cameras, and texts them along with a sound recording and your current GPS location to your emergency contact(s). The device quickly vibrates 3 times to confirm the command has been processed. If it does not vibrate, the message has not been sent, and you must try again.

Simulating a Battery Pull to Reset Your Galaxy

- Sometimes, when an Android device gets completely locked up, you need to pull the battery to restart it. However, the S7 / S7 Edge's battery is sealed inside and cannot be removed.
- There's a trick, though: press and hold the power button for 7 seconds to simulate a battery pull. It'll power off the device no matter how frozen its software is.

Making Your Galaxy Like New with a Factory Reset

- Sometimes you need to wipe your device completely—to sell it, or because it's gotten buggy and you want a fresh start.
- To factory reset your Galaxy, go to system settings → "Backup and reset" → "Factory data reset." Be warned that this permanently erases everything on your

device. Make sure you've backed up all the files you need using your apps' cloud backup features, or by copying them to your computer via USB (p. 272).

Keeping Tabs on Your Galaxy's Health with Smart Manager

- The S7 / S7 Edge include a tool called "Smart Manager" that lets you easily monitor battery life (including estimated time remaining), storage capacity, RAM usage, and device security.
- It can help you identify and delete large files in your internal storage, in the event you're running out of space. It also has a convenient "Clean All" button that deletes all caches and temporary files to keep your Galaxy running smoothly.
- It's not necessary to monitor Smart Manager all the time, but use it if you're experiencing unusual battery drain or if you need to free up extra storage space.
- Find Smart Manager in system settings → "Smart Manager."

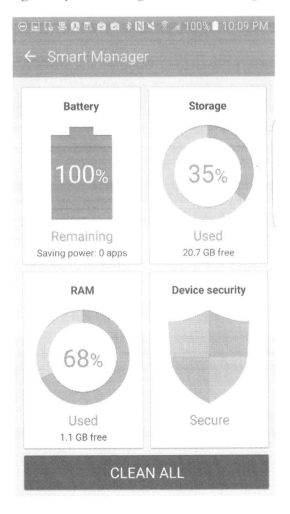

Checking for Over-the-Air (OTA) System Updates

- Android system updates, which generally only occur 1-2 times per year, are automatically delivered to you over the air. When one is available, a notification with upgrade instructions appears in your notification panel.
- If you'd like to manually check for updates, just in case, go to system settings → "About device" → "Software update." If an update is available, your Galaxy detects it and prompts you to download it.

Everything You Need to Know About Backing Up Your Data

- One of the most confusing aspects of Android is how to ensure all your data is backed up. For a new Android user, it can be very unclear what's backed up where and when, and how to restore data if needed.
- The truth is, there is no good one-stop, centralized backup solution. I think this will be a focus for Google in the next few years, but until then, you have to use a piecemeal approach, combining multiple methods. Here's what you need to know:
  - **Apps:** There is no need to back up apps downloaded from the Google Play Store. You can always re-download your apps from the Google Play Store at any time. Switching to a new Android device, or accidentally wiped your device? Just log into your Google account and follow the prompts to automatically restore all your apps.
  - **App data:** Some apps automatically back up data to your Google account. For these apps, your data is restored when the apps are reinstalled. Unfortunately, not all apps do this, and there's no easy way to know which ones do. To make sure all of your app data is backed up, use Helium Backup from the Google Play Store, or Titanium Backup (p. 277) if you root (p. 275) your device. Note, though, that relatively few apps actually contain a significant amount of user data, because frankly speaking, the majority of Android apps are designed for consuming content, not creating it. Most app data only comprise app settings that are easy to recreate and therefore not necessary to backup. Apps that do actually store large amounts of user data, such as note-taking apps or drawing apps, often have their own cloud systems that automatically back up your data. So when you're deciding whether you need an app data backup solution like Helium or Titanium, it's helpful to look through your apps one-by-one and ask yourself, "Does this app actually contain important data? If yes, does the app automatically back

it up for me over the cloud?" Usually, the answer is yes. But if not, Helium or Titanium is the way to go.

o **Text messages, Phone Logs, Settings:** Back these up using your Samsung account. Go to system settings → "Backup and reset" → "Back up my data." Turn on the sliders for the types of content you want to back up, and enable "Auto back up" so all of this data is backed up daily for you. To restore at any time, for example after your phone is wiped, just go to system settings → "Backup and reset" → "Restore."

o **Gallery Photos and Videos:** The best way to back up your camera images and videos is by using the auto-backup feature in Google's Photos app. When this feature is enabled, your Galaxy automatically uploads all photos and videos you capture to your Google account, where they are safely stored. You can view all uploaded photos and videos at any time by visiting https://photos.google.com/ on your desktop computer. To enable auto-backup, open the Photos app in your app drawer and swipe through the intro screens. Tap ☰ → "Settings" → "Back up & sync." Make sure the slider is turned on, and choose whether you want to back up on Wi-Fi networks only, or also on your cellular data connection. You also have a decision to make about photo quality; Google allows you to store an unlimited number of photos that are 16 MP or less, but any photos larger than 16 MP count toward your Google account's storage quota. Fortunately, if your Galaxy is your main camera, this is an easy decision, because its maximum resolution is only 12 MP. Therefore, you can choose the unlimited "High quality" storage option without sacrificing any quality at all. After you've configured auto-backup, your Galaxy uploads your camera media every time you take a new photo or video!

o **Gmail, Contacts, Calendar:** These are always automatically synced with your Google account—no manual steps necessary. If you lose or reset your device, the next time you log into a Google account on an Android, your Gmail, Contacts, and Calendar data are automatically restored.

o **Documents:** If you have other files on your device like Microsoft Office documents, make sure you have a cloud storage app like Google Drive (p. 250) and that you're saving all your files on your cloud drive instead of on your device's internal storage.

o **Other media (purchased songs, eBooks, etc.):** For songs, movies, eBooks, and so on, there is generally no need to backup this data. You can always re-download it from the app you bought it from (Google Play, Amazon Kindle, etc.).

Create a KNOX Device-Within-a-Device to Separate Work and Play

- Want to use your Galaxy for both personal and work use, but create a clear barrier between the two? Download the Samsung My KNOX app from the Google Play Store. This app lets you create a completely separate "virtual" environment for work use.

- You can access all your essential applications and features, but they won't have access to any of your personal data. It's like carrying two Galaxies in your pocket. For example, inside the My KNOX app you'll find the apps you're used to like Google Chrome, Gmail, Contacts, and so on, but they'll all be fresh and ready to set up with your work information—there is no overlap with the same apps outside of KNOX. Pretty handy.

Keeping Track of Time with the Always-On Display

- The S7 / S7 Edge have a new featured called "Always-On Display," which shows the time, date, and notifications on your screen even while the device is asleep. This is possible thanks to the S7's AMOLED screen, whose pixels can be turned on individually. It has a minimal impact on battery life, requiring only about 1% per hour.

- Enable the Always-On Display by going to system settings → "Display" → "Always On Display." Turn the slider to "On," and customize the other settings to your liking.

- Two warnings about the Always-On Display. First, I recommend against setting a background image. This dramatically increases the power consumption of the Always-On Display. Second, beware that the Always-On Screen only displays notifications from stock apps like Messages—not third-party apps from the Google Play Store.

Sing in the Shower Thanks to IP68 Waterproofing

- Both the S7 and S7 Edge are waterproofed to IP68 standards, which means they can theoretically withstand submersion in 5 feet of water for up to 30 minutes.

- To be clear: this doesn't mean you should purposely dunk your phone for fun, or take it into the pool for underwater photography. I don't recommend testing your phone's limits if you don't have to. But it's totally fine to use your S7 / S7 Edge in the shower, or to wash it off in the sink if it gets dirty. And if you drop it in a puddle—or worse, a toilet—everything will be just fine.

Creating Custom Ringtones

- You have two options for customizing your ringtone. The first option is to change it to one of Samsung's preloaded ringtones, by going to system settings → "Sounds and vibration" → "Ringtone."

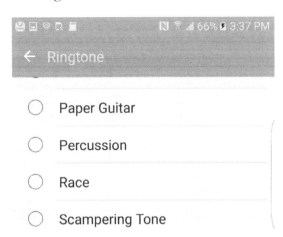

- The second option is to create a custom ringtone using your own MP3 file and the Ringtone Maker app.

- First, download an MP3 of the desired ringtone or song using a web browser on your Galaxy or transfer an MP3 by USB (p. 272). If you have an MP3 file on your desktop computer, you can also email it to yourself as an attachment and then save it using the Gmail app. It does not matter what folder you save the file to.

- Once you have an MP3 file on your device, download the app "Ringtone Maker," by Big Banc Inc. from the Google Play Store. This app lets you customize the portion of the song that plays when you get a call (e.g., the chorus).

- Once you open Ringtone Maker, tap next to the song you want to use as a ringtone. Tap "Edit."

- The following screen appears. Move the sliders around to choose the portion of the song to use for your ringtone. (Press to preview the clip, or and to zoom in and out.)

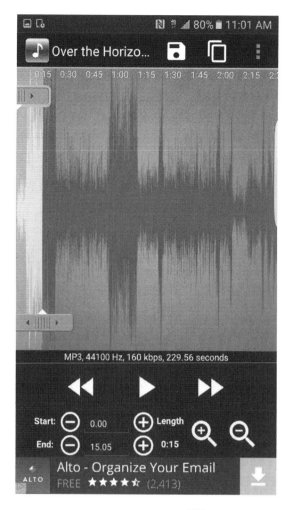

- Once you are happy with your selection, tap 🖫 to finish.
- Rename your ringtone if you wish and tap "Save." Finally, choose whether you want to make it your default ringtone for all contacts, or assign it only to a single contact.

Improving Data Performance with Smart Network Switch

- Whenever your Galaxy is connected to a Wi-Fi network, it prioritizes it over your cell data connection. This is usually a good thing, especially if you have a limited data plan. However, if you're in an area with spotty Wi-Fi coverage, your Galaxy can get stuck in a state where it's connected to Wi-Fi but has a very weak signal, making your data connection extremely slow or nonfunctional even though cell reception is good.

- So, Samsung developed Smart Network Switch, a feature that detects when Wi-Fi coverage is weak and re-prioritizes your cell connection. If you're often in a building with spotty Wi-Fi coverage, Smart Network Switch prevents a lot of frustration.
- Enable it in system settings → "Wi-Fi" → "More" → "Smart network switch."

Reviewing and Controlling App Permissions

- One of the best new features in Android 6.0 Marshmallow is increased control over app permissions. In earlier versions of Android, whenever you downloaded an app from the Google Play Store, you'd see the permissions required by the app, and you could either choose to install it or not—but you couldn't selectively block permissions. In Marshmallow, you can be as selective as you like. Don't want that app to have access to your camera and microphone? It's easy to block its access.

- In fact, there is a whole new system settings menu dedicated to managing app permissions. To use it, go to system settings → "Privacy and safety" → "App permissions." Then, tap any permission type to view and control which apps it's granted to.

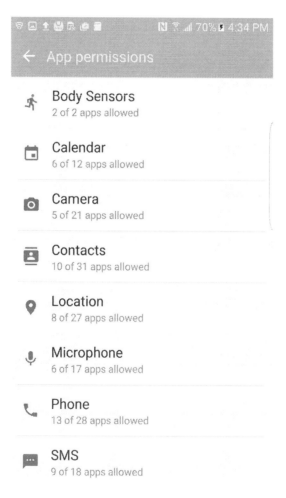

Keeping Your Screen off in Pockets and Bags

- Want to conserve battery power by making sure your screen doesn't accidentally turn on while in your pocket or bag?
- Go to system settings → "Display" and enable "Keep screen turned off." This feature takes advantage of your Galaxy's ambient light sensor to keep your battery going even longer.

Managing Default Application Behavior

- When using your Android, you might not always want web links to open in your browser—sometimes you might want them to open in their own app. For example, if you click an Amazon product while using the Chrome web browser, you'd probably rather have the Amazon product page open in the Amazon app instead of Chrome, because the Amazon app is specifically designed to give you the best Amazon shopping experience possible on Android. Or, if you click a YouTube video, you'd probably want it to open in the YouTube app, which offers many more features than the YouTube web player you get when you view a video in Chrome.
- So, Android 6.0 Marshmallow has a new Default Application manager to let you customize this behavior. Access it in system settings → "Applications" → "Default applications" → "Set as default." Tap on any app whose behavior you want to edit. Below, I'll use Amazon as an example.

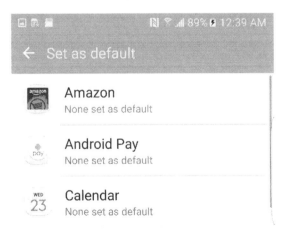

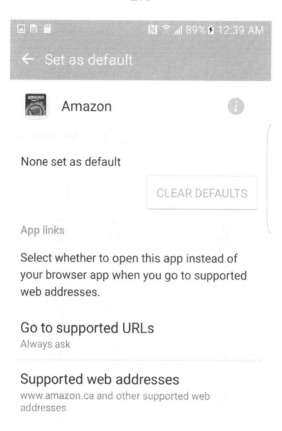

- The key field to edit is the "Go to supported URLs" field. There are three options:
  - **Via this app:** Makes the Amazon app always load all Amazon links.
  - **Always ask:** Prompt you every time you click an Amazon link, to determine whether you want to launch the Amazon app or not.
  - **In other app:** Always open Amazon links in the app in which you clicked the link. Never launch the Amazon app.
- Rarely, if ever, should it be necessary to edit the "Supported web addresses" field. Every app comes preprogrammed with its relevant web addresses, and you should never need to add any yourself.

Improving Your Android Gaming with the Game Launcher

- The Game Launcher is a new Android 6.0 Marshmallow feature that provides several different benefits:
  - A centralized "launchpad" / mini app-drawer specifically for your installed games
  - Easily disable ⬜ and ↩ buttons during gameplay
  - Easily disable alerts during gameplay

    o   Easily minimize games

    o   Easily screenshot/record gameplay

- To enable the Game Launcher, go to system settings → "Advanced features" → "Games." Turn the Game Launcher on. The Game Launcher shortcut is added to your home screen. Any games launched via the game launcher have a small red floating icon during gameplay; tap it to activate the features listed above.

Chapter 8: Advanced Functions

- By now, we've discussed nearly everything there is to know about your Galaxy, at least as it comes in the box. In this chapter, you'll learn how to extend the functionality of your Galaxy and become a bona fide power user yourself.

Connecting Your Galaxy to Your PC or Mac

Installing USB Drivers

- Some Android devices support USB Mass Storage Mode out of the box, meaning that computers automatically mount them as flash drives when connected over USB. Unfortunately, the S7 / S7 Edge are not among these devices. If you connect your Galaxy to your Windows or Mac computer via USB without first installing the proper drivers, the connection will fail.

- To remedy this situation on Windows, you need to install Samsung's USB drivers. Go to the following link and scroll down to "Manuals & Downloads." Click "Download (EXE)" to download and install the necessary USB drivers on your computer. The drivers found at the link below work for both the S7 and the S7 Edge.

http://www.samsung.com/us/support/owners/product/SM-G930TZDATMB

(Short URL: http://goo.gl/mBbO6h)

- On Mac OS, you don't need any Samsung-specific drivers, but you do need the official Android File Transfer tool:

http://www.android.com/filetransfer/

Accessing Files

- On Windows, once you have properly installed the Samsung USB drivers, you can access your Galaxy as you would a USB flash drive. Just open Windows Explorer and go to This PC → Samsung Galaxy S7 Edge.

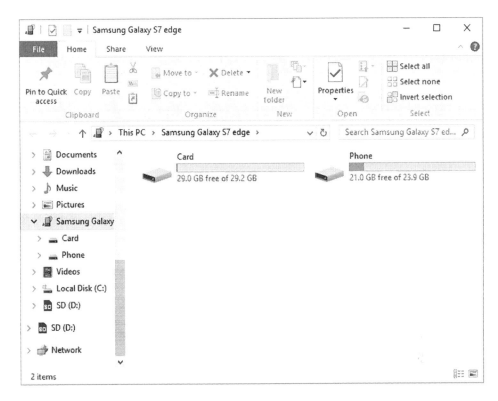

- Once you have accessed your Galaxy, open the "Phone" subdirectory to view its internal storage, or "Card" to view its external SD card, if one has been inserted. You can copy, paste, and move files just as you would elsewhere on your PC.

> **TIP:** *Be very careful about deleting or moving system or app files—only do so if you have a specific reason to and you know what you're doing.*

- On Mac OS, Android File Transfer opens as soon as you plug in your USB cable. You can drag files in and out of this window as if it were a Finder window.

⭐ **TIP:** *If your Galaxy has trouble connecting to your computer via USB, make sure USB debugging is switched off in system settings → "Developer Options (p. 238)."*

Remote Controlling Your Galaxy with AirDroid

- AirDroid is a free third-party app that lets you control your Galaxy using a web browser on your desktop computer. You can transfer files via Wi-Fi, view photos, edit contacts, manage music, view notifications, send text messages, and more. It's a very interesting and useful tool to complement basic USB connections, because it lets you go way beyond simply copying files. Plus, it's all wireless, so no cable is required.

- Download AirDroid from the Google Play Store. Install it and make sure your device is connected to the same Wi-Fi network as your computer. Start AirDroid and your device guides you through the setup process. You can create an account with AirDroid if you wish, which lets you control your device even if it's not on the same Wi-Fi network as your computer.

- I suggest you experiment with AirDroid to see how it's most useful for you. Also, consider downloading the new dedicated desktop client, which sits in your computer's system tray to provide notification monitoring and text messaging even when you don't have an AirDroid browser window open.

https://www.airdroid.com/en/get.html

Rooting Your Galaxy to Unlock More Power

!!! NOTE: At the time of publication (April 2016), there is **NO WAY** to root any **U.S. Galaxy S7 or S7 Edge models.** Samsung chose to ship the S7 and S7 Edge with locked bootloaders, which effectively prevents rooting and installing custom recoveries and ROMs. It is possible that Samsung will release a bootloader unlock utility in the future. I have left the following information in this book as reference material, but please note that it is **NOT** currently possible to root your S7 or S7 Edge. To check progress on this issue as time progresses, I suggest searching Google for "Galaxy S7 Root."

- If you've read about Android online, you've probably seen people talking about "rooting" their phones. What does this mean, and why would you want to do it?
- Android is based on Linux, and in Linux (and all Unix-like systems) the most privileged administrator account is called the "root" account. With root privileges, it's possible to execute any code you wish—code that is not normally possible to run. So, rooting your device lets you do cool stuff that's not otherwise possible.
- Here are some things you can do after rooting your device:
  - Block all advertisements in web browsers and apps
  - Share your cellular connection over Wi-Fi even if you don't pay for your carrier's hot spot option
  - Back up your apps and app data with Titanium Backup
  - Create a perfect "image" backup of your phone with Nandroid backups
  - Permanently delete bloatware
  - Replace the default operating system with a custom ROM (a version of the Android OS that enthusiasts have modified, de-bloated, or otherwise improved.)
  - … and much more.

- Note that the rooting process really comprises three separate steps:
  1. **Gaining root access itself:** This lets you do everything in the above list except install custom ROMs.
  2. **Installing a custom recovery:** A custom recovery is necessary to install custom ROMs, as well as to perform Nandroid backups (p. 277). This is optional; if you are satisfied with the stock ROM and do not need Nandroid backups, it's perfectly fine to root your device but not install a custom recovery.

3. **Install a custom ROM:** If you want to go all the way, the ultimate step in the rooting process is to install a streamlined custom ROM. Most custom ROMs are based on the stock ROM that your Galaxy ships with, but have carrier bloatware removed and additional features added. For example, many custom ROMs have call recording, battery optimizations, and so on. You may also be able to find more exotic ROMs, such as one based on the "pure" Android OS that ships with Nexus devices.

Root Warnings—Read this first!

- Before we continue further, I want to give you a word of warning. The S7 and S7 Edge have a built-in security layer called Samsung KNOX, a group of features that's targeted toward commercial and enterprise companies. To make a long story short, KNOX helps Samsung sell devices to corporate customers who need superior data security. However, if you root your device, you will trip the KNOX security flag and permanently lose KNOX features. Even if you're not a corporate user, this can affect you in several ways.
    - First, tripping the KNOX flag voids the manufacturer warranty. If you void your warranty in this way, Samsung may withhold warranty support from you in the future.
    - Second, tripping the KNOX flag permanently disables Private Mode (p. 209).
    - Third, tripping the KNOX flag permanently disables the Knox app (p. 264).
    - Fourth, tripping the KNOX flag permanently disables Samsung Pay (p. 230).

> ⭐ **_TIP:_** _When I say "permanently," I mean it. Once you've rooted your device and tripped the KNOX flag, there is no way to reset it._

- That said, thousands of users have rooted their Samsung devices and tripped their KNOX flags. Retaining the Samsung warranty is not as important as it sounds because other types of warranties and insurance plans are readily available from cell carriers themselves, and almost none of them care about your KNOX flag. As for losing Private Mode and Samsung Pay, you have to make your own judgment about whether you're willing to trade those features for the advantages of root.
- If you still want to root your device and/or install a custom ROM, continue reading.

Device Rootability

As noted above, at the time of publication, no U.S. S7 or S7 Edge models can be rooted. All rooting information in this chapter is for reference only, and will apply to the S7 and S7 Edge only if Samsung chooses to release a bootloader unlock utility.

	S7	S7 Edge
Sprint	No	No
T-Mobile	No	No
AT&T	No	No
Verizon	No	No

If you're interested in rooting your S7 or S7 Edge, I suggest periodically searching Google for "Galaxy S7 Root" to see if there's any recent news about a root method.

Root Instructions

[Redacted due to the S7 and S7 Edge shipping with locked bootloaders]

Things to Do After You've Rooted Your Galaxy

Imaging your Device with Nandroid Backups

- Nandroid backups are a special and powerful type of backup, and are only possible when you've rooted *and* installed a custom recovery. A Nandroid backup creates an exact image of your device's internal memory and compresses it into a single folder. This lets you freely tinker and experiment with your device, because you can always quickly and easily revert to a fixed "last known good state" using a Nandroid backup folder.
- To create a Nandroid backup (assuming you've already installed a custom recovery), you need to boot into recovery by restarting your Galaxy while holding the Volume Up + Home + Power buttons. Use the "backup" and "restore" options of your custom recovery to back up your data. If you want to store your Nandroid backups for safekeeping, you can copy them to your computer's hard disk via USB.

Backing Up Apps and App Data with Titanium Backup

- Titanium Backup lets you backup and restore your apps and app data to a single folder. It's most useful when you're installing a new custom ROM—it's easier to backup and restore your apps using Titanium Backup than to re-download everything from the Play Store, and you are sure to not to lose any app data.

(Google's new <u>Tap & Go restore system</u> (p. 34) could eventually give Titanium Backup a run for its money, but not until it properly and reliably backs up ALL app data like Titanium Backup does.)

- The free version of Titanium Backup performs basic backups and restores but purchasing a pro key gives you many more options ($5.99 on the Google Play Store).

- Before using Titanium Backup for the first time, you need to enable USB debugging. To do so, go to system settings → "About device." Double-tap on "Build number" repeatedly and a notification appears that developer options have been enabled. Go back to system settings, tap "Developer options," switch the slider in the upper-right-hand corner of the screen to "On," and enable "USB debugging."

> ⭐ ***TIP:*** *In some cases, enabling USB debugging can prevent a proper USB connection with your computer. If you have trouble connecting over USB after enabling USB debugging, disable it again.*

- To perform a backup with Titanium Backup, tap ☑ → "Run" next to "Backup all user apps."

- Select the apps you wish to back up and then tap ☑. This backs up all your apps and associated data.

- By default, you'll find your backed up apps in the /Card/TitaniumBackup/ folder when you connect to your Galaxy via USB. Remember to copy this folder to your computer for safekeeping, if desired.

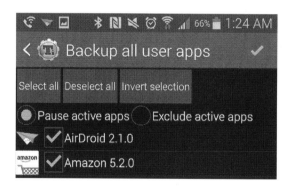

- To restore a backup, use the "Restore missing apps with data" option. Here, you can select whether to restore apps with data, apps only, or data only.

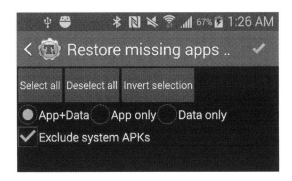

WARNING: *It's okay to restore apps and app data when moving to a new custom ROM, but you should never restore system data on a new custom ROM, or you will cause a multitude of errors and have to start over from scratch.*

- That's all there is to it—unless you want to use any of Titanium Backup's other features, which are numerous. If so, I suggest consulting the official documentation here:

> *http://www.titaniumtrack.com/kb/titanium-backup-kb*

Blocking Ads with AdAway

- Blocking ads is one of the best things you can do after you've rooted. There are several apps designed for this purpose, but I have found AdAway to be the best. It blocks advertisements everywhere on your device—in the stock browser, in Chrome, and in apps.

- AdAway is not on the Google Play Store; it is on an alternative platform called F-Droid. Download F-Droid at the link below and install it to your Galaxy. Search for "AdAway" in F-Droid and install it by tapping the latest version number at the bottom of the screen. Open AdAway, tap the button entitled "Download files and apply ad blocking." Reboot your device when the process is done, and it will be ad-free!

> *https://f-droid.org/*

Tethering Your Internet Connection for Free

- Another advantage of rooting is that you can use Wi-Fi tethering without paying your carrier's hot spot fees.

> **WARNING:** *Although your carrier has no way of knowing with certainty that you are tethering, you will set off alarms if you use a massive amount of bandwidth. I advise against using this method to stream video or download large files. Use it for regular web browsing and you will be fine. Of course, I take no responsibility for your actions if you choose to violate the terms of your contract.*

- **The best way to do this is to install a custom ROM that features "unrestricted native tethering."** A ROM like this lets you use the built-in tethering feature in system settings → "Mobile HotSpot and Tethering."
- If you cannot find a suitable custom ROM, or you want to have unlimited tethering on a rooted stock ROM, the next best option is to use the third-party tethering app called **WiFi Tether Router**, available for $2.50 from the Google Play Store. This app can generally be made to work, although sometimes it is finicky, which is why it is not my preferred solution. Purchase and install this app. Open it and tap "Configure WiFi Router." You may see a message about "Scan always available." If so, tap OK, uncheck "Always allow scanning," and then tap ↰ to return to the app.
- Enter the following settings:
    - **Network Name SSID:** *Your choice*
    - **Encryption Type:** wpa2-psk
    - **WiFi Password:** *Your choice*
    - **WiFi Channel:** 1
    - **Interface:** wlan0
    - **Method:** 3- HostApd
    - **No Firmware Reload:** Unchecked
    - **Drivers:** nl80211
    - **WiFi Mode:** G
    - **Keep Screen ON:** Unchecked
    - **Prevents Stand-By:** Checked
- Tap ↰ to save these settings.
- If you have T-Mobile, go to system settings → "Mobile networks" → "Access Point Names" → "Add." Enter the following settings:
    - **Name:** T-Mobile Tethering
    - **APN:** fast.t-mobile.com
    - **Proxy:** Not set
    - **Port:** Not set
    - **Username:** Not set
    - **Password:** Not set

- o **Server:** Not set
- o **MMSC:** http://mms.msg.eng.t-mobile.com/mms/wapenc
- o **Multimedia message proxy:** Not set
- o **Multimedia message port:** Not set
- o **MCC:** 310
- o **MNC:** 260
- o **Authentication type:** Not set
- o **APN type:** default,supl,mms
- o **APN protocol:** IPv4
- o **APN roaming protocol:** IPv4

- Tap ⤺ to save these settings, then change the radio button to select the new APN.
- Next, go to system settings → "Wi-Fi." Tap any known networks and "Forget" them. Make sure your Wi-Fi is on, but you're not connected to any networks. Now, go back to WiFi Tether Router and tap "Enable WiFi Router." If all settings are correct, your Galaxy creates a new network with the specified SSID.
- Finally, download a user agent spoofer for your desktop browser of choice, and set it to an Android device. This step is very important, because without it, your carrier can still detect you're using a desktop browser. If you use Chrome, this is a good spoofer:

> *https://chrome.google.com/webstore/detail/user-agent-switcher/ffhkkpnppgnfaobgihpdblnhmmbodake/related?hl=en*
>
> *(Short URL: http://goo.gl/bfMhPR)*

Automating Tasks with Tasker

- Tasker is one of the most powerful and unique Android apps available. It lets you program your Android to do almost any automated task you can imagine. Want your Galaxy to disable Wi-Fi and start playing music when you get in your car? No problem. Want it to automatically download and apply a new wallpaper every day? You can make it happen. Tasker has almost unlimited power but the learning curve is steep.
- To learn how to use Tasker, I suggest starting with this YouTube channel:

> *https://www.youtube.com/playlist?list=PLjV3HijScGMynGvjJrvNNd5Q9pPy255dL*
>
> *(Short URL: http://goo.gl/RZdj7S)*

Overclocking Your Galaxy with Custom Kernels

- Want to overclock (or underclock) your Galaxy's CPU? You can do this with a custom kernel. Once you have rooted and installed a custom recovery, download a custom kernel from your carrier's page on XDA (look in the "Original Android Development" sub-forum). Make sure you do your research first—don't fry your Galaxy by changing settings you don't understand.

Getting Inverted Apps and Other Mods

- If you have rooted and installed a custom recovery, you can install "flashable ZIP" mods. Flashing a ZIP mod is basically flashing a single feature you might find on a custom ROM. For example, in your device's sub-forum on XDA, you might find a flashable ZIP to enable call recording. Another popular one is inverted stock apps—a mod that turns light-colored app backgrounds to black. This is easier on the eyes and on your device's battery.
- To find flashable ZIP mods, look for posts tagged "[MOD]" in the "Themes and Apps" sub-section of your device's XDA forum.

DON'T Accept Over-the-Air Updates

- If you root your Galaxy without installing a custom ROM, you will still receive notifications of new over-the-air updates from Samsung or your carrier. You must not install these updates, or you'll likely lose root.
- Furthermore, if the update patches the root exploit, you may not be able to get root back until a new exploit is developed. Take care not to sabotage your efforts by applying an OTA update to your rooted Galaxy.

Unrooting

- Unrooting is easy: just download a stock ROM from your carrier's sub-forum on XDA and flash it using ODIN.
- Note that this does NOT reset your KNOX flag—there is no way to reset a tripped KNOX flag.

Using NFC Tags to Quickly Perform Tasks

- One cool and little-known feature of the S7 / S7 Edge is their compatibility with Samsung's TecTiles 2 tags. These are tiny 1x1" stickers with embedded RFID chips. You can place them around your home, car, or office and program them to do different tasks when you tap your phone on them. For example, you might stick one on your car's dashboard and program it to toggle GPS, open the Maps app, and start playing music.

- You can buy TecTiles 2 from Samsung.com, Amazon.com, or similar online retailers.

- To use TecTiles 2, download and install the Samsung TecTiles app from the Google Play Store. Follow its instructions to program your TecTiles 2. Make sure NFC is turned on or your device will not detect TecTiles 2 tags when you tap it against them.

- Personally, my most-used TecTile 2 is one on the wall next to my bed. I have a night and a normal profile, and my TecTile 2 switches between them. At night, I tap my Galaxy to decrease the brightness, silence it, and open the Clock app so I can set an alarm. In the morning, I tap my Galaxy on the same TecTile 2 to turn up the brightness, and turn my ringer on again.

> **TIP:** *Make sure you purchase TecTiles 2, not the original TecTiles. The originals are incompatible with the S7 / S7 Edge.*

Using a USB OTG Cable to Connect USB Devices

- USB OTG (On-The-Go) is another little-known feature of Android and is fully supported on the S7 and S7 Edge.

- Purchase a USB OTG adapter like the one linked below, and you'll be able to connect USB flash drives, mice, keyboards, game controllers, and other USB devices to your Galaxy. It is even possible to use USB OTG in conjunction with a USB hub to connect multiple devices at the same time.

---

http://www.amazon.com/dp/B00871Q5PI

- If connecting a USB flash drive, use a file browser like Solid Explorer (p. 307) to view and copy files.

Saving Battery Power

- At various points in this book, I have made suggestions about how to conserve battery power. Here, I have consolidated them all for you and added some additional information.

- In general, the greatest source of power consumption on Android devices is the screen. On the S7 / S7 Edge, you will notice a massive difference in battery life depending on the brightness setting you use. If you're having battery life woes, this is the first thing to check. I find that on my Galaxy, even 20% brightness is more than enough for comfortable usage except in bright sunlight.

> **TIP:** *The S7 and S7 Edge have Super AMOLED screens, which do not have a backlight. Rather, the brightness of each individual pixel is individually controlled. This means that it takes less power to display darker colors. One trick to reduce your screen's power consumption is to use dark wallpaper and set apps to use dark themes when possible.*

- The second greatest source of battery drain is apps themselves. In general, your battery life will decline as you install more apps—and to some degree, this is normal. If you are installing apps that perform background services, which many do, they require power.

- However, many apps are poorly coded and drain much more than their fair share of battery power. Try to only install reputable apps (p. 168), and if your battery is draining faster than it should, uninstall or disable apps you're not using. Battery drain is less of a problem in Android 6.0 Marshmallow than it used to be, however, thanks to Google's new automatic Doze feature that limits apps' background activity.

- You can view estimates of battery usage by app in system settings → "Battery" → "Battery usage." If you're having a serious problem and can't seem to find the culprit, your only option may be to factory reset your Galaxy and install apps a couple at a time until you identify the offender.

- Here are some additional ways to reclaim battery life:
  - Use Power Saving Mode and Ultra Power Saving Mode (p. 239) when possible.
  - Use Wi-Fi instead of cellular networks when possible; the Wi-Fi radio requires much less power. Some people think that turning Wi-Fi off saves battery life throughout the day. This is not true. If you are connected to a Wi-Fi network, your Galaxy consumes less power than if you were connected to a 4G LTE network.

o   As mentioned above, use dark wallpaper for your home screen and lock screen.

o   Delete unused widgets from your home screens and disable unused features in system settings.

o   Disable the "Location" toggle button in the notification panel when you don't need GPS or other location detection.

o   Disable Bluetooth in the notification panel when you don't need it.

o   For apps that regularly connect to the Internet, check their settings menus to see if you can reduce the frequency with which they check for updates.

o   Buy a high-capacity aftermarket battery pack from a site like Amazon.com. Read about these in Chapter 11 (p. 311).

o   Avoid "task killer" apps like Juice Defender. These apps don't actually save battery power, and sometimes they even consume more.

o   Install a third-party launcher like Nova Launcher (p. 303) to disable the battery-draining parallax motion effect that occurs when you tilt your Galaxy on the home screen or app drawer. Unfortunately, there's no way to disable this effect in the stock launcher.

o   Enable "Keep screen turned off" in system settings → "Display."

TIP: *Advanced users may want to check out BetterBatteryStats ($2.16 on the Google Play Store). It has a steep learning curve beyond the scope of this book, but is a very powerful tool for determining what is draining your battery.*

Keeping Your Battery Healthy

•   To make your battery last as long as possible in the long run, try to run it down to ~10% every couple weeks—but try not to go much lower, and if you must, charge it up as soon as possible thereafter. It's okay to run it down to 10% more often— just don't let it drain all the way and sit idle for an extended period of time, because doing so will eventually ruin your battery. If you treat your battery properly, it should last for as long as you own your Galaxy.

TIP: *Use the included charger to charge your Galaxy when possible. Your Galaxy can absorb four hours of juice in just 10 minutes using Adaptive Fast Charging.*

Online Resources / Getting Help with Your Galaxy

- There are numerous Android-related online communities, but two of my favorites are Android Central and XDA. Android Central is an excellent source of Android news and reviews, while XDA is my preferred source for all things related to rooting and customization. The site has dedicated forums for each of the major carriers:

> *Galaxy S7:* *http://forum.xda-developers.com/galaxy-s7;*
> *http://forums.androidcentral.com/samsung-galaxy-s7/*
>
> *Galaxy S7 Edge:* *http://forum.xda-developers.com/s7-edge;*
> *http://forums.androidcentral.com/samsung-galaxy-s7-edge/*

- Either of these websites is a good place to ask for help with your Galaxy—but in my experience, XDA is a better place to seek help with troubleshooting and anything related to rooting.

Chapter 9: Preloaded Apps

Good work. By now, you know more about your Galaxy than 99% of other users—but we're not done yet.

In this chapter, I give you a quick rundown of the apps that come preloaded on the S7 / S7 Edge. I tell you what each one does—often it's unclear without experimentation—and provide my commentary on overall usefulness and potential alternatives. The S7 and S7 Edge include some very good and interesting apps, but they also include some "bloatware," junk apps that Samsung gets paid to include but are not the best options available.

NOTE: Depending on your cell carrier, you may be missing one or two of the apps in this section, or you may have some extra apps not mentioned here. This is completely normal. This chapter contains the core list of stock apps, but each carrier has the final say on what comes preloaded on their phones.

Amazon

Normally, I'd complain about a shopping app being preloaded on my phone, but come on… it's Amazon. I love Amazon. You love Amazon. You probably bought this book on Amazon. And, the Amazon app is actually one of the best e-commerce apps on Android. It's fast, responsive, and unlike many of its competitors, isn't missing any features. In many ways, it's actually superior to browsing Amazon on the web thanks to its streamlined interface. Personally, I prefer the app to the website when placing orders with Amazon.

Furthermore, the S7 / S7 Edge come with the full Amazon App, which includes the Amazon Appstore. The full Amazon App isn't available on the Google Play Store—Google only offers the "Amazon Shopping" app which excludes the app store component—because Google prohibits apps on the Play Store from having their own built-in app stores. The Amazon App normally has to be downloaded separately from Amazon's website, so it's a nice bonus that it's included.

Note that the Amazon app is not for reading Kindle books, listening to Amazon Music, or watching Amazon Instant Video. Amazon has separate apps for these services. You can get the Kindle and Prime Music apps from the Google Play Store (p. 166), but you need to get the Prime Instant Video app from the Amazon App.

Android Pay

Android Pay is Google's tap-to-pay payment system. Like Samsung Pay, the basic idea is that you register your credit or debit card and then pay at credit/debit terminals using your phone. However, Android Pay only supports paying at NFC terminals, which are generally only found at select convenience stores, fast food joints, and vending machines. Most major retailers and small businesses do not have NFC-enabled terminals.

Samsung Pay, on the other hand, supports both NFC and magnetic swipe terminals. And of course, magnetic swipe terminals are ubiquitous, which means Samsung Pay lets you pay just about everywhere.

So, Samsung Pay is strictly superior to Android Pay. Android Pay is the only game in town if you have a non-Samsung phone, but since you have an S7 with Samsung's LoopPay magnetic swipe technology, there is no reason whatsoever to use Android Pay. Stick with Samsung Pay.

Briefing

Briefing is a news and social media aggregator based on the Flipboard app. It combines your news and social media feeds to create a personalized "magazine." By default, it's accessed by swiping left from the main home screen. I'm personally not a fan of its flashy "magazine" interface, and I don't like how easy it is to accidentally open on the home screen. I recommend disabling Briefing (p. 249), and using gReader (p. 301) instead for your RSS needs.

Calculator

A very basic calculator. Works fine, but I recommend RealCalc (p. 305) if you want a scientific calculator.

Calendar

Samsung's Calendar app, discussed at length here (p. 161). This app is sometimes called "S Planner" in Samsung's product documentation. If you don't like the Samsung Calendar for any reason, try downloading the official Google Calendar app from the Google Play Store. However, I personally think the Samsung Calendar is more attractive and intuitive than the Google Calendar.

Camera

For capturing photos and video, and discussed at length here (p. 123). Although there are alternative camera apps available on the Google Play Store, I strongly recommend sticking with the stock app, as it's quite powerful and is optimized for your Galaxy's hardware. It is possible to find alternative camera apps on the Google Play Store, but you'll find that photos taken with them are much lower quality than photos taken with the stock Camera app.

Chrome

The Android version of Google's popular Chrome web browser. Discussed at length here (p. 98). Chrome is my Android web browser of choice, for its speed and ability to sync bookmarks, open tabs, and history with my desktop computer.

Clock

Samsung's stock Clock app, discussed here (p. 145). Includes a timer, stopwatch, world clock, and alarms. If you're looking for a more beautiful and full-featured clock app, try Timely from the Google Play Store.

Contacts

Samsung's stock phone book, discussed here (p. 138).

Drive

Google Drive is a cloud storage app. It lets you upload, back up, and download files to and from an online hard drive, and synchronize your files across multiple devices. Clients are available for multiple operating systems, including Windows, Mac OS, and Android.

In general, I am a huge advocate of cloud storage services. I used to use Dropbox, but I now use Drive because it provides more free storage space and integrates with my Google account. Drive is a critical part of my workflow. I save all of my personal and work files to Google Drive folder while using my computer. This way, they're always available on my Galaxy and on any computer that has Internet access.

In addition to keeping your files backed up and available on the cloud, Drive also saves every single version of your files, so you can revert to previous versions if you accidentally overwrite a file. This has been invaluable for me and many other users.

If you aren't using a cloud storage service, pick one and start now. I suggest Google Drive. Read more about Drive here (p. 250).

Email

A generic POP3/IMAP email client; nothing special. The Gmail app (p. 115) now supports non-Gmail POP3 and IMAP email accounts, so I suggest using it instead of the Email app if you have a non-Gmail email account you want to set up on your Galaxy. The Email app is obsolete, a vestige from older versions of Android.

Facebook

The official Facebook app for Android. Connects you with friends and family who use the Facebook social network. Notorious for causing battery drain and device slowdown. If you don't use Facebook, I strongly recommend disabling (p. 252) this app. Unfortunately, there is no credible 3ʳᵈ party alternative, so if you're a big Facebook user, you'll just have to make do. The only possible alternative is using the mobile Facebook site through your web browser, but it's much more limited than the app.

Galaxy Apps

Galaxy Apps is Samsung's app store. I recommend avoiding Galaxy Apps and getting all your apps from the official Google Play Store or Amazon app store (p. 169) instead. That way, all your Android apps will be available to you in the future, whether or not you have a Samsung phone. Also, apps in Samsung's app store aren't always kept up to date, and the selection of apps is extremely limited compared to the Google Play Store.

That said, some free software updates (e.g., voice synthesis files, camera modes, themes, etc.) must be downloaded from the Galaxy Apps store, so I don't recommend disabling it.

Gallery

For viewing and editing photos and videos. Discussed at length here (p. 133). If you don't like the stock Gallery app, try downloading Focus from the Google Play Store.

Gmail

Gmail is Google's official Gmail Android app. Used for sending and receiving mail with your Gmail account. The best Gmail client available, truly a great app. Discussed at length here (p. 115).

Google

This app should be called "Google Now," because that's all it is—a shortcut to Google Now (p. 174). Note that on previous Android devices, Google Now was accessed by pressing and holding ⬭, but in Android 6.0 Marshmallow, pressing and holding ⬭ launches Now on Tap (p. 181) instead. In Marshmallow, the Google app is the primary way to open Google Now, so this app is more useful than it was in the past.

Hangouts

Hangouts is the mobile app for Google's chat platform—the same one you see when you're logged into Gmail on your computer. Hangouts is a fine app and Google has improved it a lot since it came out. It does not significantly drain your battery while running and works very well for text or video chatting with your contacts. If you use Gmail chat a lot, Hangouts is the best app to chat on the go.

> ⭐ **TIP:** *Hangouts now also supports SMS (text messaging) and MMS (picture messaging). If you want to use Hangouts instead of Messages for texting, open it and go to ☰ (in upper left corner) → "Settings" → "SMS" and enable SMS.*

Internet

The stock Android web browser. I recommend using Chrome (p. 98) instead, because it syncs with the desktop version of Chrome and is updated more frequently. However, Internet does have some perks, like the ability to save web pages for offline viewing and to auto-fill login information using the fingerprint reader. Additionally, some users claim that Internet is faster than Chrome. Like I said, I recommend Chrome for maximum integration with your desktop browser, but Internet isn't a bad choice if Chrome doesn't float your boat.

Lookout

Lookout does three things: 1) antivirus, 2) backup of your Google contacts and photos, and 3) allows you to locate your phone by GPS if you lose it.

In my opinion, Lookout is the best all-in-one Android security app available… but despite that, it's unnecessary and redundant.

- The anti-virus feature is unnecessary as long as you adhere to my best practices (p. 168) when downloading new apps. I've never used an antivirus app on Android, and I've never gotten a virus. Research apps before you download them, the way I teach you to, and you'll never get a virus either.
- The backup function is redundant because your Google contacts are already automatically backed up with Google, and you should be using Photos's automatic photo backup (p. 262) to back up your photos directly to your Google account instead of to Lookout's website.

- The device-locating feature is helpful, but you can already locate your device using Android Device Manager (p. 208), or if you want even more powerful features, Cerberus (p. 298) (my personal favorite).

I consider Lookout to be bloatware because it targets users who are misinformed and/or scared of nonexistent threats. It's designed to suck you in so you'll pay the monthly subscription fee. As long as you know what you're doing—which you do, by now—you don't need Lookout. I suggest disabling (p. 252) it.

Maps

The Android version of Google Maps. An amazing app—the only one you'll ever need to navigate. Discussed at length here (p. 151).

Memo

A basic note-taking app. Not bad, but not a great choice because it lacks a backup mechanism. If your phone is lost or wiped, you'll lose everything in the Memo app. Furthermore, there's no easy way to share your memos with your desktop computer. I recommend using Evernote (p. 300) instead, which features automatic cloud backup and has PC/Mac clients available.

Messages

The stock app for sending text messages (SMS) and multimedia messages (MMS). I personally like it a lot. If you don't, popular alternatives on the Google Play Store include Textra, Chomp SMS, and Go SMS. As I mentioned earlier, you can also now use Hangouts (p. 290) as your SMS client.

My Files

My Files is a file manager. It lets you access the file system of your Galaxy.

My Files works fine but it is inferior and limited compared to the excellent and free Solid Explorer (p. 307). Solid Explorer has a better interface, allows root (p. 275) access to file directories, and is frequently updated. Ditch My Files and don't look back. The one exception is that you need My Files to view files you've hidden using Private Mode (p. 209).

Phone

The stock dialer. It's possible to replace it (check out ExDialer on the Google Play Store), but I usually stick with the stock dialer myself. Discussed here (p. 103).

Photos

The Photos app is essentially Google's version of Samsung's Gallery app. It lets you browse and view photos saved on your Galaxy. However, unlike the Gallery app, it also displays photos that are saved to your Google Photos account online, and can be configured to automatically upload all camera photos to your Google account. This is an *amazing* feature that ensures you never lose any photos you take.

All photos automatically uploaded by the Photos app can be accessed at:

> *https://photos.google.com/*

I strongly suggest configuring Photos to upload all your pictures to your Google account. Read here (p. 262) for instructions on enabling auto-backup.

Play Store

The official source for downloading new apps for your Galaxy. Discussed here (p. 166). An indispensable app. The second biggest app store is the Amazon app store (p. 169).

Play Movies & TV/Music

These apps let you buy and consume media from Google. Although only Play Movies & TV and Play Music come preloaded on the S7 / S7 Edge, you can download the other Play apps free from the Play Store, including Play Games, Play Books, and Play Newsstand.

The Play apps work well, have reasonable prices, and have a large selection. Whether you use them or not will likely depend on the degree to which you've already bought into other platforms. For example, I read all of my eBooks on my Kindle, so I buy eBooks exclusively from Amazon and never from Play Books. Similarly, if you are already invested in iTunes, you might not want to buy music from Google Music. But if you're not already invested anywhere else, Google Play is not a bad platform on which to start a media collection. The situation you want to avoid is buying a bunch of media on one platform and then switching to another platform later, causing your media collection to be fragmented across different platforms. Read more here (p. 184).

S Health

S Health offers several tools to track and maintain your fitness, including a pedometer, a GPS tracker for running, a food tracker, a weight diary, and more. See more information on S Health here (p. 243).

S Voice

S Voice is Samsung's personal assistant. It offers most of the same features as Google Now (p. 174), but unlike Google Now, doesn't have a card system. A couple years ago, S Voice actually outperformed Google Now in terms of capabilities and voice recognition accuracy, but Google Now has come a long way while S Voice has stagnated. As of 2016, Google Now is clearly superior to S Voice. Read more here (p. 181).

Samsung Gear

Samsung Gear is the companion app for Samsung Gear smartwatches. If you buy one, use this app to connect it to your Galaxy. If you don't have a Gear Smartwatch, this app doesn't do anything.

Samsung Milk Music

Milk is Samsung's streaming music service. It allows you to listen to dozens of different curated "stations" in multiple genres. It's free to listen, but there are some limitations. You have to endure between-song ads, you can't listen offline, and you can only skip a limited number of songs per hour. To remove these restrictions, you can sign up for a subscription for $3.99 per month.

In my opinion, there are much better options on the market than Milk. Namely, Google Play Music All Access. It costs more than Milk ($9.99 per month), but it has a huge catalog and lets you stream anything you want, at any time, with almost no limitations. Read more here (p. 147).

Samsung Pay

The Samsung Pay app lets you configure Samsung Pay, Samsung's new tap-to-pay payment service. Lets you register your credit and debit cards with your Galaxy, so you can use your S7 to pay at nearly any credit/debit payment terminal. Very amazing technology, and probably my favorite feature on the S7. Read more about Samsung Pay here (p. 230).

Samsung+

The Samsung+ app gives you one-touch access to Samsung customer support (including live video chat), app recommendations, Galaxy tips & tricks, and more. While you probably won't use Samsung+ on a daily basis, I would recommend checking it out because it does have some valuable content, especially for first-time Galaxy owners. Note that you must sign into a Samsung account to use this app.

Settings

The system settings app. Same as swiping down the notification panel (p. 75) and tapping ✿ . Discussed here (p. 63).

YouTube

Lets you stream videos from YouTube, the biggest video site on the Internet.

Chapter 10: The 50 All-Time Best Android Apps

Below is a list of my all-time best app recommendations, taken from my book, *The 50 All-Time Best Android Apps*. Some are free and some are paid. I am in no way affiliated with any of the developers, and I stand to gain nothing from your purchases. My recommendations come from my own experience and research. http://www.amazon.com/dp/B00L8ES1L2

1Weather

1Weather is an attractive, functional weather app. It contains all the weather information you need, including hourly, daily, and weekly forecasts. It also offers real-time weather mapping, sunrise/sunset information, and push notifications to keep you informed of changing conditions. Plus, you can easily switch between cities when you travel. In my opinion, no other Android weather app comes close to 1Weather's functionality, style, and simplicity.

Price: Free from the Google Play Store / $1.99 in-app purchase to remove ads

AirDroid

AirDroid offers a unique way to control your Android device—using a web browser on your desktop computer. After you have installed the app on your Android, you just go to http://web.airdroid.com/ in your browser to open the control panel (or install the AirDroid utility on your computer). From there, you can view photos and videos, change your ringtone, manage contacts, send and receive text messages, listen to music on your Android device, transfer files, take screenshots, and more.

In this way, AirDroid is good for many things—mass updates of your phone book with the convenience of a keyboard, showing photos on a big screen, transferring files wirelessly instead of over a USB cable, texting on your computer, and more.

Price: Free from the Google Play Store / $1.99 per month for premium

Amazon

The Amazon app has two components: 1) online shopping and 2) the Amazon Underground app store. Prior to 2014, the Amazon Appstore was a separate app, but it's now integrated with the e-commerce Amazon app. And with the Amazon Underground, Amazon is offering more free apps than ever. This 2-in-1 value means that the Amazon app is one of the all-time best. The Amazon app is a must-have, and best of all, it's preloaded on the S7 and S7 Edge.

Read more about the Amazon Underground <u>here</u> (p. 169).

Price: Free, preloaded

Audio Recorder by Sony

Curiously, Samsung chose not to include a voice recording app on the S7 / S7 Edge. I recommend Sony's Audio Recorder app to fill the void. It's easy to use, records high-quality audio, requires minimal permissions, and is totally free.

Price: Free from the Google Play Store

Authenticator

Google Authenticator is a two-factor security solution that works with many websites that require a password login, including Gmail, Dropbox, LastPass, and Evernote.

What is a two-factor security solution?

With Authenticator, anyone who logs into your (Gmail, Dropbox, LastPass, Evernote, etc.) account is required to input a code generated by Authenticator in addition to the password. This way, even if someone steals your password, they are not able to log into your account without also having physical possession of your Android. Authenticator even works when your device has no Internet connection. The biggest downside is that only a select few websites support it.

Once you're comfortable using Authenticator, consider downloading the "Authy" app from the Play Store. It's like a beefed-up version of Authenticator that backs up all your 2-factor keys online, so if you lose or reset your Galaxy, you won't risk getting locked out of your accounts.

Price: Free from the Google Play Store

Barcode Scanner

Barcode Scanner allows you to scan barcodes and QR codes. I use it to comparison shop at the store, to quickly pull up product reviews, and to scan QR codes. Barcode Scanner also happens to be required for some features in Authenticator.

Price: Free from the Google Play Store

Boson X

Boson X is one of the few Android games that has stood the test of time for me. It is a unique arcade-style game with a fantastic soundtrack. It's easy to pick up and play when you only have a few minutes to kill, but deep enough to keep you occupied for hours if you want. Not many games strike this balance as well as Boson X.

Price: $2.99 from the Google Play Store

Call Recorder by skvalex

Have you ever wanted to record voice calls on your Android phone? Although quite expensive at $9.95, Call Recorder by skvalex is the best call recording app available and is capable of recording to both WAV and MP3. Plus, root (p. 275) access is not required. But before recording any calls, make sure you're aware of the wiretapping laws in your jurisdiction.

Price: Free trial from http://goo.gl/u690rm / $9.95 to buy on the Google Play Store

Cerberus Anti Theft

Most "Best App" lists say that Lookout is the best Android anti-theft app available, but I disagree. Cerberus is my security app of choice. Unlike Lookout and most other phone-locating security apps, Cerberus has absolutely no monthly fee—only a one-time purchase of $4. Better yet, it doesn't slow down your phone, doesn't drain your battery, works reliably, and can even hide itself from the app drawer. Its online control panel is simple and streamlined and works every time. Additionally, unlike Android Device Manager (p. 208),

Cerberus lets you remotely control your Galaxy via text message—which work even when your phone is outside of data coverage. I trust Cerberus more than any other app to help me retrieve my Galaxy should I ever lose it.

Price: Free trial from the Google Play Store / ~$4 in-app purchase to buy

Chipotle

No, this is not a joke! For a long time, Chipotle only had an iOS app and they did a poor job of announcing the Android app when they finally released it, so I want to spread the word. The app is well-designed, easy to use, and most importantly, allows you to order online and go straight to the register to pick up your order. No more waiting in line. Any app that can save 20-30 minutes of my day is a winner. If you don't eat at Chipotle but you do eat at other quick serve restaurants, see if they have a similar app on the Google Play store that let you skip the line. Many do.

Price: Free from the Google Play Store

Cloud Print

Want to wirelessly print from your Galaxy? Cloud Print is an official Google app that lets you do exactly that. You just install a Chrome extension on your desktop computer, register your printer with Google Cloud Print, install the Android app, and you're set. No printer drivers or complicated wireless settings needed. The Android app lets you print documents, photos, PDFs, and more. You can also print directly from mobile Chrome or any app that supports the Share Via (p. 94) tool. Read more here (p. 248).

Price: Free from the Google Play Store

eBay

eBay's mobile app is free and much better than its slow and buggy mobile website. In the past, the official app was inferior to a third-party app called Pocket Auctions, but it's come a long way since then. It supports all major features, including search filters, best offers, PayPal payments, and so on. If you're a regular eBay user, get it now. You'll also want to grab the free PayPal (p. 304) app for additional PayPal features beyond auction payments.

Price: Free from the Google Play Store

Evernote

Evernote is a cross-platform cloud note-taking app, and supports both Windows and MacOS in addition to Android. How many of us just email notes to ourselves, or scrawl them on the backs of napkins? Evernote is a much easier and more secure way of keeping notes organized and synchronized between devices. Any note you save into Evernote is automatically backed up in the cloud and copied to your other devices, so you'll never lose data or be without your notes. I use Evernote for shopping lists, journaling, organizing notes for my books, brainstorming, and more. And unless you store a ton of images or audio recordings in your notes, you'll be totally fine with the free service.

Price: Free trial from the Google Play Store; desktop version available at https://evernote.com **/ Premium service $5 per month**

Fenix for Twitter

I used to recommend Talon for Twitter, but it's defunct now. With Talon gone, I believe Fenix is the best option. It's stable, well-designed, and functional. Of all the Twitter apps I've tested, it's what I always come back to.

Price: $4.49 from the Google Play Store

Google Drive

Google Drive is so much more than a simple app. Drive gives you cloud storage space, where you can upload and store files from your computer or mobile device. (And if you weren't already aware, you already have a Drive account if you have a Gmail account. Access it at http://drive.google.com.)

The benefits of using Drive are threefold. First, any files saved on your Drive are backed up. If your computer hard drive crashes or you lose your Galaxy, any files saved to your Drive will survive. Second, since you can access Drive via your computer or the app on your Galaxy, your files are available no matter where you are. Forget to email yourself a file? No problem—as long as your desktop computer has the Drive software installed and you saved the file to your Drive, you can get it with the Android app. Third, Drive saves every version of every file. Accidentally overwrite your thesis? Just log into the web interface and roll back the file.

Personally, I have the Windows/Mac desktop Drive software and the mobile app, and I save all my work files to my Drive folder. This way, I never lose data and I am never without my data.

In the past, I recommended Dropbox instead of Drive. However, Google now offers significantly more free space than Dropbox (15 GB vs. 2 GB), and its software is just as good. If you aren't already using Drive, start today.

Price: Free from the Google Play Store

Google Rewards

Google Rewards is a free download from the Google Play Store that gives you Play Store credit in exchange for filling out market research surveys. When you first install the app, you fill out some demographic information, and then whenever you fit the profile for a survey that Google is running, you get a notification in your notification tray. It takes a minimal amount of time to respond to these surveys and you can earn $50+ per year doing it—often times enough to cover all of your Google Play purchases. Just be honest with your responses—Google employs a variety of techniques to screen your answers, and if they think you're trying to game the system, they'll stop sending you surveys.

Price: Free from the Google Play Store

gReader

gReader is an RSS news reader that synchronizes with a Feedly account to bring all your news to your Galaxy. If you aren't familiar with RSS feeds, here's what you need to know: RSS feeds are files that contain recent posts from their respective websites. Most news websites and blogs publish them. When you import them into an RSS reader like Feedly, they let you read news from multiple sources all in one place without visiting many different websites. It's fast and convenient. gReader is simply an app for using your Feedly account on your Galaxy

If you want the best-looking RSS app, you might prefer the official Feedly app or Pulse. But for a functional, no-nonsense RSS reader with plenty of functions like offline reading, gReader is the way to go. There's a free version, but the paid version removes ads and provides extra features like better widgets and voice dictation of articles.

Price: Free trial from the Google Play Store / $4.69 to buy

GTasks

Many Android devices (including the S7 and S7 Edge) don't come with a good to-do app, and where those apps do exist, they generally don't sync with Google Tasks. GTasks is a simple to-do list that solves this problem. If you want a simple to-do list that you can access from both your Galaxy and your Gmail account on your computer, GTasks is the way to go. It has a nice, simple interface, and it has never failed to save and synchronize my tasks.

Price: Free trial from the Google Play Store / $4.99 to buy

Key Ring Reward Cards & Coupon

Key Ring stores all of your loyalty and shopping rewards cards. Don't let those frequent flyer miles go to waste! Better yet, it allows you to easily share cards with other Key Ring users and access weekly fliers and coupons that cashiers can scan right from your phone's screen. The one downside is the in-app ads, and there is no premium version to remove them.

Price: Free from the Google Play Store

Kitchen Timer

Kitchen Timer corrects the one-timer-at-a-time deficiency found in the stock Clock (p. 145) app. Kitchen Timer allows you to set up to three timers at once and doesn't require any unusual installation privileges. It's a great, bare-bones app and is completely free. I use it all the time when I'm cooking multiple dishes at once.

Price: Free from the Google Play Store

LastPass

LastPass is a cross-platform password manager. I use it extensively on my desktop to autofill personal information and credit card numbers, generate random passwords, and store my login info for everything. The Android client is a must-have because it makes all your passwords available on the go, and has an excellent helper app that can autofill login information in any app. If you're looking for a password manager, I highly recommend LastPass. I used to use Dashlane, but LastPass has been improved a lot in the last year, and offers a better experience for a lot less money.

Price: Desktop client is free from https://lastpass.com/, Android client is free from the Google Play Store; subscription (which is necessary for cloud syncing to Android) is $12/year

MX Player

MX Player is my favorite video player. The built-in Video app is sufficient if you only watch short clips, but if you watch a lot of movies, TV shows, or files in obscure formats, MX

Player provides a much better experience. It also handles subtitles like a champ. The paid version removes ads.

Price: Free trial from the Google Play Store / $5.99 to buy

Mycelium Bitcoin Wallet

If you don't know what Bitcoin is, you can skip this app. If you do, all you need to know is that Mycelium is the best Bitcoin wallet for Android. It has features that other apps don't, such as full BIP38 paper wallet support, and it's open source so you can be confident it's safe to use. I always keep some bitcoin in my Mycelium wallet in case I stumble upon a store or restaurant that accepts it.

Price: Free from the Google Play Store

Netflix

If you have a Netflix subscription, the Netflix app is a must-have. If you don't have a Netflix subscription… what are you thinking?!? Netflix is one of the best services in today's economy, period. The value is… amazing. Get a subscription so you can watch amazing video like Breaking Bad, House of Cards, Sherlock, Law & Order, and more. Early adopters of the S7 / S7 Edge can even get a <u>free year of Netflix</u> (p. 237).

Price: Free from the Google Play Store (Netflix streaming subscription required)

Nova Launcher

Nova Launcher is a highly customizable home screen replacement. If you're tired of the stock TouchWiz look, then try Nova Launcher. You can customize the number of rows and columns for the apps displayed on each screen, margins, scroll effects, shadows, your app tray, and much more. You can even hide apps from your app drawer.

Price: Free trial from the Google Play Store / $4.00 to buy

Pandora

Pandora is a music streaming service. Its library of songs is much smaller than Spotify's and it doesn't let you play specific songs, but it's a great resource for discovering new music similar to what you already like. I don't pull up Pandora when I want to hear a specific song, but rather when I want to hear something new. Pandora is free, but you can only skip 6 songs per hour and you have to endure ads unless you pay for the premium service. I don't really recommend subscribing, though—your money is much better spent with Google Play Music All Access (p. 147). Take what you get from Pandora's free service and run with it.

Price: Free from the Google Play Store / subscription service $4.99 per month

PayPal

If you use PayPal for personal payments or business, the Android app is a must-have. It's much faster and easier than using the full PayPal site on a mobile browser and supports most common functions. (Though, it does not have the ability to create a custom invoice, which I would like to see added.) I use it to square up restaurant checks with friends and family, to make online purchases, and to take payments for my business.

Price: Free from the Google Play Store

Play Music

Although Google Play Music is not as powerful as some other third-party MP3 players, the features of the Play Music ecosystem nevertheless make it the best way to listen to your music collection on the go.

Why? Google allows you to upload up to 20,000 of your own songs to the cloud—for free—which are then available to stream on your Galaxy via the Play Music app, from your web browser, or from any public computer. This allows you to have your entire MP3 collection available on-demand through your Galaxy, without requiring any storage space. But don't worry—if you want to download music for offline playback, Play Music makes that easy, too.

Moreover, if you subscribe to Google Play Music All Access, the Play Music app lets you stream unlimited music, on-demand, with no restrictions. Plus, All Access comes with free YouTube Red. Overall, Play Music is an amazing and free service and is the absolute best way to take your music collection with you. Read more here (p. 148).

Price: Free from the Google Play Store / Download Google Play Music for Chrome from https://support.google.com/googleplay/answer/4627259?hl=en

Pocket

Pocket offers a one-click solution to save articles for later. It's two parts: An Android app and a desktop Google Chrome extension. Whenever you come across a web page on your desktop that you want to read later, you just hit the Pocket button and the web page's text is instantly sent to your Pocket app for on-the-go reading later. Pocket is great because it's just so darn easy to use.

Price: Free from the Google Play Store

Pocket Casts

Pocket Casts is, in my opinion, the best podcast app for Android. It does a magnificent job of managing, filtering, downloading, and playing your podcasts, and can even back up your settings to the cloud.

Price: $3.99 on the Google Play Store

Pushbullet

Pushbullet has 2 parts: an Android app and a Chrome desktop browser extension. When both are installed and configured, all notifications on your Galaxy are mirrored on your desktop computer, and you can even browse and reply to texts from your computer. Pushbullet is a must-have, because when you're sitting at your computer, it's far more convenient to see notifications on your monitor and reply to texts with your keyboard than to pick up your phone every time it sounds a notification.

Pushbullet's functionality somewhat overlaps with AirDroid (p. 274), but is a great choice if you don't need all the extra features of AirDroid. Personally, I have both installed on my Galaxy. I use Pushbullet on a daily basis because it's lighter weight and runs transparently in the background, and I start up AirDroid whenever I need device management features beyond just notifications and texting.

Price: Free from the Google Play Store

RealCalc

RealCalc has a nicer interface than the stock Calculator app and offers scientific functions. It also supports RPN mode and allows for a great deal of customization. The paid version adds more features such as fraction conversions, landscape mode, and support for degrees and minutes. It's my preferred Android calculator app.

Price: Free trial from the Google Play Store / $3.49 to buy

Reddit is Fun

If you read Reddit, I highly recommend Reddit is Fun. It's a much better way to browse Reddit than using a mobile browser and has all the features you could possibly want. There are a few other Reddit readers on the Google Play Store, but in my experience Reddit is Fun is the best of them.

Price: Free trial from the Google Play Store / $1.99 to buy

Ringtone Maker

Ringtone Maker does exactly what it sounds like: it lets you edit MP3s and other audio files to create custom ringtones and easily assign them to contacts on your phone. It's much easier to use Ringtone Maker's all-in-one package than to try to use a separate music editor and figure out how to set the resulting file as a ringtone in OS settings. Ringtone Maker is absolutely free and adds a feature that should be, but rarely is, included by default on Android smartphones. Read more here (p. 265).

Price: Free from the Google Play Store

Robinhood

Robinhood is a stock-trading app with a big twist: no fees. That's right—with Robinhood, you can buy and sell stocks without paying a dime. The company makes money by collecting interest from customers who upgrade to margin accounts, and from collecting interest on uninvested account balances.

Price: Free from the Google Play Store

Scanner Radio

This app is awesome. It allows you to live stream police and emergency services radio frequencies to your Android. If you are in close proximity to an emergency response, you often can tune into the local frequencies and find out what's going on first-hand. Sometimes, you can even hear foot chases and other criminal pursuits as they happen.

Price: Free trial from the Google Play Store / $2.99 to buy

Screen Adjuster

Screen Adjuster is a small, free app that allows you to set your screen's brightness below the normal minimum level. It's very useful in dark environments to avoid losing your night vision or to avoid distracting other people in public venues like movie theaters. I use it before bed to minimize the impact of my Android's screen on my melatonin levels. Science!

Price: Free trial from the Google Play Store / $0.99 to buy

SMS Backup & Restore

This app allows you to backup and restore your SMS and MMS messages to your Galaxy's SD card or to Dropbox. It works seamlessly and quickly unlike many other text message backup apps. I highly recommend using it to back up your messages or to transfer them to a new phone. (Note: you can also use your Samsung account to back up text messages (p. 262).)

Price: Free trial from the Google Play Store / $3.49 to buy

Snes9xEX+

This app is an excellent and free Super Nintendo emulator. After you have downloaded ROM game files from the Internet, you can load them into SNES9xEX+ and play them exactly as they were on the original console. (Legal caveat: you must own the original cartridges to legally download ROM files.) Remember Super Mario World, Zelda, and Final Fantasy II/III? Great games—play them with Snes9xEX+.

The author of Snes9xEX+, Robert Broglia, sells emulators for most other classic gaming consoles as well. Snes9xEX+ is the free one that hooks you. The rest cost money, but they're all excellent apps.

Price: Free from the Google Play Store

Solid Explorer

Solid Explorer is a full-featured file manager. Although Android does not prominently feature a file and folder storage system like on desktop computers, these things do exist behind the scenes and Solid Explorer lets you access them. It's much more powerful than the "My Files" app that comes with the S7 / S7 Edge, and I recommend it wholeheartedly for copying, moving, renaming, and deleting your files.

Price: Free from the Google Play Store

Speedtest

Speedtest is a free app that tests the speed of your Internet connection, be it Wi-Fi or cellular. It's useful to help diagnose connectivity problems, or just to show your friends how much faster your 4G LTE cell connection is than their home cable connection.

Price: Free from the Google Play Store

SuperBeam

SuperBeam is the best way to perform blazing-fast wireless file transfers between Android devices. SuperBeam uses Wi-Fi Direct but implements it a lot more effectively than the Android OS does. When two Android phones have SuperBeam installed, they are on the same page—end of story. There's no messing around with complicated device settings like Android Beam or Wi-Fi Direct. I strongly recommend you use SuperBeam to transfer large files between Android devices.

Price: Free trial from the Google Play Store / $1.99 to buy

TeamViewer

TeamViewer is a cross-platform screen-sharing program. You set up the client on your desktop computer and then access and control it from your Android phone. Yes, this means you can control your computer's screen right from your Android device! It works very well, even over slower connections. TeamViewer is incredibly cool and useful, and best of all it's completely free for personal use.

Price: Free from the Google Play Store; desktop client available at http://www.teamviewer.com/

TeslaLED

TeslaLED is a free flashlight program that's brighter than the built-in Flashlight (p. 253) toggle. It includes several handy widgets for quickly turning your camera flash LED into a flashlight. I also really like that it doesn't request any unusual permissions at installation.

Price: Free from the Google Play Store / $1.00 optional donation

TouchDown For Smartphones

TouchDown is the best Microsoft Outlook replacement, bar none. It has all the built-in features of Outlook including Mail, Calendar, Tasks, and so on. If your work uses Exchange,

TouchDown is simply an excellent way to keep up with your work on the go. Moreover, because it consolidates all the functions of Outlook into a single app, it creates a very nice barrier between your work life and your personal life. It's not cheap, but if you use Outlook it's well worth it.

Price: Free trial from the Google Play Store / $19.99 to buy

TuneIn Radio

This app allows you to stream local and national AM/FM radio stations over the Internet. It's very useful for listening to radio stations in other parts of the country, for example while traveling. It can also be useful for tuning in to local stations when your regular radio reception is poor but you have a good Internet connection.

Price: Free trial from the Google Play Store / $9.99 to buy

Uber

Unless you've been living under a rock for the last year, you've probably heard about Uber. It's a new taxi/private car/rideshare service that competes with traditional taxi cabs (and has been the target of a lot of lawsuits from taxi unions). Instead of flagging down a taxi on a city street or calling a dispatcher, you just launch the Uber app and request a ride. The wait is usually short and the drivers professional. Payment is made through the app, and no tip is required or expected, making Uber cheaper than most regular taxis. Uber operates in medium-to-large cities in 57 countries.

Price: Free from the Google Play Store

WhatsApp Messenger

Don't have unlimited texts? No problem. Get WhatsApp and get your friends to do the same. It uses a proprietary network to send and receives text-based messages without burning through your SMS quota. There are a lot of services like WhatsApp, but it has my recommendation because it is the most popular one and your friends and family are more likely to already have it.

Price: Free from the Google Play Store

Wikipedia

The Wikipedia app is a fast and lightweight way to read Wikipedia articles on your Galaxy. For me, there's one key reason it's better than accessing the mobile website through a browser: its ability to invert colors so you can read white text on a black background. Not only is this easier on the eyes, it's also easier on battery life.

Price: Free from the Google Play Store

ZArchiver

ZArchiver is an archive manager compatible with a huge array of file types, including .zip, .rar, .7z, and many, many more. It is very fast, lightweight, and completely free.

Price: Free from the Google Play Store / $1.30 optional donation

Chapter 11: Accessory Shopping Guide

There is a wide range of accessories available for the S7 and S7 Edge. In this chapter, I provide examples of both official and third party accessories to give you an idea of what's available. I also recommend specific accessories that I have experience with.

Please note that there are hundreds, if not thousands of accessories already available for the S7 and S7 Edge, and it would be impossible to cover them all here. If you're interested in any of the accessories I discuss in this chapter, you should do your own research to compare prices and brands. For example, many of the official Samsung accessories I discuss have off-brand alternatives that may be just as good and/or cheaper. And, the products I link to may be cheaper from other vendors. This chapter is only a starting point.

> ⭐ **TIP:** Register your Galaxy on Samsung's website to receive a coupon good for 30% off any mobile accessory $59.99 or less.
>
> http://www.samsung.com/us/support/register/product
>
> After registering, you'll receive an email entitled "Your gift for registering your Galaxy," containing your coupon code for the Samsung store, linked below.
>
> http://www.samsung.com/us/mobile/cell-phones-accessories

Cases

There are several categories of cases for the S7 and S7 Edge. The most general and widely appealing type is the **TPU case**. TPU cases are flexible but firm plastic. They hold their shape extremely well and resist stretching over time. TPU cases only became popular in the last few years, but they're a huge step up from the old cheap rubber cases that caught on fabric and easily got stretched out.

I've been using Spigen's Thin Fit TPU case ($10 street price) and I like it a lot for its slim profile and affordable price. Spigen makes Thin Fit models for both the S7 and the S7 Edge:

> *S7: http://www.amazon.com/dp/B01A7ICRLO*
>
> *S7 Edge: http://www.amazon.com/dp/B01A7IDCC2*

These cases offer a great balance of slimness, grip in the hand, price, and protection. They easily slip in and out of a pocket but aren't slippery in the hand.

Similar TPU cases are available from most carriers' retail stores, although you'll likely pay 2-3 times what you would pay for an online brand like Spigen.

Sometimes you can find cases shaped like the Spigen but made of **hard plastic**. These are common on eBay and usually sell directly from Asia for 3-4 dollars shipped. However, I recommend TPU instead because of its grippy texture and because it won't crack.

Another alternative is the **S-View Flip Cover** ($60 street price), which provides more functionality but less protection. It flips open and closed like a book cover, and while closed, lets the Galaxy display information such as the time and date through the case.

S7: *http://www.amazon.com/dp/B01B1WBBPS/*

S7 Edge: *http://www.amazon.com/dp/B01B1WB93C/*

If you want something really heavy duty, the **OtterBox Defender** ($50 street price) is a good solution. It provides *excellent* protection including a built-in screen protector. However, it's big—really big. It makes the Galaxy seem absolutely massive, actually. But the protection it offers is second-to-none. Plus, the word is that OtterBox is using a new formulation for the outer shell, making it tougher and more stretch-proof than ever before.

At the time of writing, the Defender is only available for the S7, but there is a slimmer OtterBox called the **Commuter** ($30 street price) that provides tough protection for the S7 Edge while also showcasing its design.

S7 Defender: *http://www.amazon.com/dp/B00Z7SGZTA/*

S7 Edge Commuter: *http://www.amazon.com/dp/B00Z7TFCAC/*

Other types of cases are available but less common, such as belt holsters, pouches, kickstand cases, and even wooden cases. Amazon and eBay are good starting points to find something more unusual.

> **TIP:** *The S7 and S7 Edge have different dimensions than previous Galaxy devices, so if you have cases for the S5, S6, S6 Edge, etc., you won't be able to use them with your new Galaxy unless they're loose-fitting.*

Micro SD Memory Cards

The S7 and S7 Edge mark the return of the Micro SD memory card slot to the Galaxy S line, after their disappointing absence on the S6 and S6 Edge. Good thing, too, because the S7 and S7 Edge are only available with 32 GB of internal memory, unlike many earlier Galaxy S models which were available with 64 GB and 128 GB.

Micro SD cards expand the capacity of your Galaxy to store music, photos, videos, and other data. And these days, they're dirt cheap.

I recommend Samsung's Class 10 EVO cards (street price 32 GB $10 / 64 GB $20 / 128 GB $40):

http://www.amazon.com/dp/B00IVPU786/

The biggest and beefiest Micro SD card currently in production is SanDisk's Ultra 200 GB (street price $80):

http://www.amazon.com/gp/offer-listing/B00V62XBQQ/

See installation instructions here (p. 27).

Cables & Connectivity

Audio/Video Connectivity

To stream music, photos, and video from your Galaxy to your TV, you should purchase a Google Chromecast. It works amazingly well for wirelessly streaming all kinds of content—music, videos, and photos—and is only $35.

https://www.google.com/chromecast/buy-tv/

Be aware that the S7 and S7 Edge are not compatible with common MHL-to-HDMI adapters, or older Samsung AllShare Cast devices.

Data/Charging Cables

Many new Android phones are shipping with next-gen USB-C ports, but the S7 and S7 Edge have standard Micro USB 2 ports. A little disappointing on one hand, but it does make cable shopping easier.

I suggest using the included cable whenever possible, because it has a thick enough wire gauge to support Adaptive Fast Charging (p. 254). If you need an additional cable, look for a "USB-A to Micro USB cable" that supports "Quick Charge 2.0." If you get a cable that's not rated for QC2.0, it may not charge your phone at the maximum possible speed.

Also, consider picking up an inexpensive USB OTG cable to connect your Galaxy to flash drives, mice, keyboards, and more ($1.50 street price).

http://www.amazon.com/dp/B005GI2VMG/

Read more about USB OTG here (p. 283).

Headsets

The S7 / S7 Edge support both wired and Bluetooth wireless headsets. (Most carriers include a basic wired headset in the box.) Samsung sells a variety of both, although Amazon has a larger selection and lower prices. Learn how to pair a Bluetooth headset here (p. 215).

If you're looking for a basic Bluetooth headset, I recommend the Plantronics M55 ($20 street price).

http://www.amazon.com/dp/B00815AB00/

Batteries & Chargers

The S7 and S7 Edge are very power-hungry devices, yet at the same time their battery life is impressive. To accomplish this, they use power-efficient architecture with huge 3,000/3,600-mAh batteries, respectively, charged by 2.0 amp chargers with Adaptive Fast Charging technology. Translation? Long battery life and super-fast charging.

The included power brick is much more powerful than typical smartphone chargers and outputs far more current than any computer's USB port, so for optimal charging times you should always charge with the provided charger through a wall outlet. Note that generic 2.0 amp chargers from other devices will *not* charge as quickly as the stock charger with the Adaptive Fast Charging capability.

> ⭐ **TIP:** *The generic name for Samsung's "Adaptive Fast Charging" technology is "Quick Charge 2.0." Any charger labeled as Quick Charge 2.0 will charge your Galaxy just as fast as the original Samsung charger.*

One downside of the S7 and S7 Edge is that they don't have removable batteries, so you can't pick up a spare like you could for previous Galaxy models. However, you can pick up a USB battery pack like this Choetech, which supports Quick Charge 2.0 and recharges your Galaxy multiple times. I keep one in my backpack and it often comes in handy.

http://www.amazon.com/dp/B00ZCGLBT6/

Wireless Chargers

The S7 and S7 Edge have built-in support for industry standard Qi- and PMA-compatible wireless charging pads. Wireless charging isn't nearly as fast as wired Adaptive Fast Charging, but it's a lot more convenient on a desk. I have the following Anker charger ($15) and it works great:

http://www.amazon.com/dp/B00Y839YMU/

If you're willing to shell out a little more ($70), you can pick up Samsung's Fast Charge wireless pad, which is compatible with both the S7 and S7 Edge. It charges your Galaxy about 40% faster than a standard charging pad. Still not as fast as wired Adaptive Fast Charging, but close.

http://www.amazon.com/dp/B012AWBN9C/

Car Chargers

Any standard car charger with a micro USB connector will charge your Galaxy, but low-current chargers won't provide much juice. Go for a Quick Charge 2.0-compatible unit like this Powermod ($16 street price):

http://www.amazon.com/dp/B00P9UILUM/

Bluetooth Speakers

Cheap, standalone battery-powered Bluetooth speakers are becoming very popular, and they pair nicely with the S7 / S7 Edge. Examples include the Oontz Angle 3 ($30 street price) and the DKnight Magicbox II ($35 street price). I personally have the Magicbox II and I love it.

> *Oontz: http://www.amazon.com/dp/B010OYASRG/*
>
> *DKnight: http://www.amazon.com/dp/B00NXET2MM/*

These units are about the size of a smartphone, but thicker. They're much, much more powerful you're your Galaxy's internal speaker, and have a battery life in the 10-hour range. These little speakers are great for when you need a little (or a lot of) extra volume. More expensive variants exist, like the Bose SoundLink Mini ($199 street price), but the price-to-performance ratio of the cheaper units is impressive.

Screen Protectors

There are countless brands of screen protectors, some of which are only a couple dollars per pack. However, I suggest springing for more than the bare minimum quality. The S7 and S7 Edge have some of the best screens of all time—why would you cover them up with a hazy screen protector?

My favorite protectors for the S7 are Spigen's Crystal protectors ($10 street price). These are super clear and are a great value for the money.

> *S7: http://www.spigen.com/collections/galaxy-s7/products/galaxy-s7-screen-protector-crystal*

If you want the absolute best quality and clarity possible, go for Spigen's tempered glass protectors ($25 street price):

> *S7: http://www.spigen.com/collections/galaxy-s7/products/galaxy-s7-screen-protector-glas-tr-slim-hd*

For the S7 Edge, try Spigen's curved Crystal protectors ($25 street price). Note that some S7 Edge screen protectors don't properly cover the screen's edges, so be careful if you purchase an alternate brand:

> *S7 Edge:* *http://www.spigen.com/products/galaxy-s7-edge-screen-protector-curved-crystal*

Unfortunately, Spigen doesn't make curved tempered glass protectors for the S7 Edge. It is possible to find off-brand curved tempered glass protectors online, but in my experience they aren't worthwhile.

Vehicle Docks

Samsung sells a Universal Vehicle Navigation Mount for the Galaxy series ($30 street price), which is compatible with both the S7 and S7 Edge. It's useful both improving hands-free access, and/or using your phone as your main GPS.

> *http://www.amazon.com/dp/B0089VO7HE*

Another popular and cheaper option is the iOttie dashboard mount ($20 street price):

> *http://www.amazon.com/dp/B007FH716W/*

Home Lighting

Have you heard of Philips Hue or LIFX bulbs? They're the two most popular Wi-Fi home LED lighting systems, and they're smartphone-controlled. Both systems' apps are compatible with the S7 / S7 Edge, so there has never been a better time to get some fancy new lighting for your place. Both systems offer millions of colors including a full white spectrum, programmability and timers, and more. Find them on Amazon and read reviews on Google to determine which system is best for you.

Smartwatches

Smartwatches are becoming a big business. The S7 and S7 Edge is compatible with most of the major types, including Android Wear, Galaxy Gear with Tizen OS, Pebble, Sony, and more. You'll have to do your own research if you want to get the best watch for your purposes, but I personally own a Pebble, Android Wear, and a Sony Smartwatch 2 and I prefer the Pebble for its long battery life and to-the-point functionality.

Other Accessories

Other accessories include, but are not limited to:

NFC TecTiles 2: These are programmable RFID stickers. You can place them around your home, car, and office, and execute custom actions when you tap your Galaxy against them. The S7 and S7 Edge are only compatible with TecTiles 2. Read more about TecTiles here (p. 283).

Various Other Peripherals: Bluetooth keyboards, etc.

My Other Books

If you enjoyed this book, you might be interested in purchasing some of my other recent books.

Samsung Galaxy Note 5 & S6 Edge+: The 100% Unofficial User Guide

http://www.amazon.com/dp/1517272750/

Samsung Galaxy S6 and S6 Edge: The 100% Unofficial User Guide

http://www.amazon.com/dp/1511935421/

Samsung Galaxy Note 4: The 100% Unofficial User Guide

http://www.amazon.com/dp/1505391385/